VICTORIOUS IN BATTLE

VICTORIOUS IN BATTLE

BELIEVING, SPEAKING, AND ACTING ON GOD'S WORD

SIMONE JOOSTE

Without limiting the rights under copyright(s) reserved below, no part of this publication may be reproduced, stored in or introduced into a retrieval system, or transmitted, in any form, or by any means (electronic, mechanical, photocopying, recording, or otherwise) without the prior permission of the publisher and the copyright owner.

The content of this book is provided "AS IS." The Publisher and the Author make no guarantees or warranties as to the accuracy, adequacy or completeness of or results to be obtained from using the content of this book, including any information that can be accessed through hyperlinks or otherwise, and expressly disclaim any warranty expressed or implied, including but not limited to implied warranties of merchantability or fitness for a particular purpose. This limitation of liability shall apply to any claim or cause whatsoever whether such claim or cause arises in contract, tort, or otherwise. In short, you, the reader, are responsible for your choices and the results they bring.

The scanning, uploading, and distributing of this book via the internet or via any other means without the permission of the publisher and copyright owner is illegal and punishable by law. Please purchase only authorized copies, and do not participate in or encourage piracy of copyrighted materials. Your support of the author's rights is appreciated.

Scriptures marked KJV are taken from the KING JAMES VERSION KJV: KING JAMES VERSION, public domain.

Scripture quotations marked (NLT) are taken from the *Holy Bible*, New Living Translation, copyright ©1996, 2004, 2015 by Tyndale House Foundation. Used by permission of Tyndale House Publishers, Carol Stream, Illinois 60188. All rights reserved.

Scripture quotations are from the ESV®Bible (The Holy Bible, English Standard Version®), copyright© 2001 by Crossway Bibles, a publishing ministry of Good News Publishers. Used by permission. All rights reserved.

Scripture quotations taken from the Amplified® Bible AMPC, Copyright © 1954, 1958, 1962, 1964, 1965, 1987 by The Lockman Foundation. Used by permission. www.Lockman.org"

Scripture quotations taken from the Amplified® Bible (AMP), Copyright © 2015 by The Lockman Foundation. Used by permission. lockman.org"

Scripture quotations marked (NIV) are taken from the Holy Bible, New International Version®, NIV®. Copyright © 1973, 1978, 1984, 2011 by

Biblica, Inc.™ Used by permission of Zondervan. All rights reserved worldwide. www.zondervan.comThe "NIV" and "New International Version" are trademarks registered in the United States Patent and Trademark Office by Biblica, Inc.™

Copyright © 2024 by Simone Jooste. All rights reserved.

Released: December 2024
ISBN: 978-1-64457-773-8

Rise UP Publications
644 Shrewsbury Commons Ave
Ste 249
Shrewsbury PA 17361
United States of America

www.riseUPpublications.com
Phone: 866-846-5123

Dedicated to my husband, Tim, who has taught me to be strong, leading by such an amazing example. To our two children, Eva and Judah. Take all that we have done, and go further than we ever could with the equipping you have been given.

"Now every athlete who goes into training conducts himself temperately and restricts himself in all things. They do it to win a wreath that will soon wither, but we [do it to receive a crown of eternal blessedness] that cannot wither."

1 CORINTHIANS 9:25 AMPC

CONTENTS

Introduction	13
Chapter 1 *Eva*	17
Chapter 2 *Repetition Reaps Results*	29
Chapter 3 *The Attack*	39
Chapter 4 *The Battle*	49
Chapter 5 *The Victory*	59
Chapter 6 *The Weapon*	71
Chapter 7 *The Testimony*	93
Chapter 8 *Sound Mind*	101
Salvation	113
About the Author	115

INTRODUCTION

I wrote this book for anyone facing a battle in their life and feels stuck in defeat, doesn't see a way out, and feels like hope and happiness are beyond reach. God doesn't want you to stay in a place of defeat; He wants you to live a life of victory in Him.

My own battle followed a miscarriage, and writing a book was not in my plans at this stage of my life, but I felt God's call to share my story and insights. Too many believers go through hardships and remain in a state of defeat, but God desires for us to be victorious. If this book helps even one person transition from defeat to victory, it will have been worth it. Remember, going through a battle doesn't mean you are meant to stay there. How you respond will determine your outcome.

I tell my kids, "Life isn't about what happens; it's about how you respond to it." Every day, we have a choice to fight or succumb to our situations. A few years ago, I had a revelation that impacted my life greatly: *Sometimes life is just hard, but*

INTRODUCTION

you can choose your hard. Sometimes, doing hard things reaps the greatest results.

Everyone defines "hard" differently; it's anything that isn't easy for you personally. What is hard for others might be a walk in the park for you. We are all in different places spiritually, mentally, emotionally, and physically. Just because you are strong in one area doesn't mean you are strong in all areas—you will have your own battles to face.

A business owner has different challenges than an employee. The challenges of a poor person differ from those of a wealthy person. *And* being wealthy doesn't exempt you from challenges. Challenges come to everyone, but *you* can choose your hard.

Being fit isn't easy; it takes hard work and determination. You must decide to get up early and workout, and choose not to eat certain foods, even if that means skipping a meal sometimes. It requires dedication and discipline. Similarly, when an unexpected challenge comes, you must decide to face it head-on.

My pastor says when you expect life to be easy, it's hard. But when you anticipate challenges and prepare yourself for them, life gets easier. For some people, everything is a big deal. But when you are spiritually and mentally equipped, big things become smaller. If you want to advance, take territory, or progress in life, you will have to level up and get stronger. People who seek an easy life full of comfort often find themselves in uncomfortable situations and are not prepared to handle them. **Seeking an easy life will not be a life of satisfaction**. But saying, "I may be challenged, but I'll never be defeated," prepares you for a life of victory.

INTRODUCTION

We have many great examples in the Word of God of living *victorious in battle* amid challenging situations. King David killed Goliath, and the children of Israel overcame giants in their promised land. Abraham and Sarah overcame old age to receive their miracle child. You might face an obstacle, but that does not mean God isn't with you. Just as it was for David, the obstacle in front of you is an opportunity to move up higher.

As children of God, we are supposed to go from glory to glory, victory to victory, strength to strength, and faith to faith. If you have faced a battle in any area, I pray you feel strengthened in your inner man to fight. We refer to it as "being in the Lord's army" for a reason. There is a fight. And with the right equipping, you can, and will be, victorious!

CHAPTER ONE

EVA

Eva's Birth Story

I want to start by sharing my daughter's birth story. I want you to see a life of victory, not a life of battles and struggles. We go from victory to victory and strength to strength. For my story, this is the perfect place to begin. I pray you are encouraged as you read this; knowing what God did for me, He is willing and able to do for you in any area of your life.

In 2015, my husband and I were ready for our first child, and had been married for seven years. When I was very young, about eight to ten years old, I heard my mom mention supernatural childbirth. At that moment, I knew I wanted to believe God for a supernatural birth. And as I got older, I became interested in a more natural and holistic approach to health and living. I learned about some of the unnecessary medical practices that happen during childbirth and throughout the medical industry as a whole. Not to mention all the harmful additives in foods. As much as this interested me, I knew I couldn't focus on the natural birth process. Instead, I needed to focus on the supernatural way made available through the Blood of Jesus and His precious sacrifice.

I studied what happens naturally, but focused on the supernatural. I read the book *Supernatural Childbirth* by Jackie Mize, and I listened to the audiobook repeatedly. My mom had the original tape Jackie references in the book, and put it on a CD for me. My husband worked long hours, so I played the audiobook or CD when making dinner, or any chance I got. I wrote out my own confessions pertaining to what I was believing for, and recorded myself speaking them. They covered conception, pregnancy, labor and delivery, peace, and rebuking fear. Everyday, I declared the confessions, knowing God's peace was *my* peace.

I knew God designed my body to get pregnant, carry my baby to full term, and deliver and nurse my baby. I learned natural childbirth was possible, and is the way God intended for us to give birth. He designed childbirth to be enjoyable and wonderful.

Learning information in the natural was important, but the most powerful thing I learned was that life and death are in the power of the tongue (Proverbs 18:21).

 Whatever I said is what I would have, and fear would be my greatest enemy.

Speaking fear or doubt of any kind would hinder me from achieving my goal, so there could be no room for fear in my life. I had to have complete faith and reliance on God's Word, knowing what He said was true. My faith was built up in this area, and I knew I would receive what I believed for. This was more than head knowledge, it was a heart revelation. I *knew* with my spirit what Jesus did, and my part was to act. Faith acts on the truth of God's Word!

I aggressively protected who I spoke and listened to, and this is important for you to note. If I knew someone wouldn't understand what I was believing for, I wouldn't have that conversation with them. You can't speak faith and doubt at the same time. You also can't have others around, who believe contrary to what you are believing for.

When you are pregnant, everyone wants to tell you their negative experiences, but you *do not* have to listen. You can gently direct the conversation in another way.

 I protected my ears, thoughts, and beliefs.

This works in any area where you are believing God for something. It may seem extreme to avoid people and conversations, but what I believed for was too precious, and I had to protect it.

 Only you can protect your dreams, desires, and calling. It's not anyone else's responsibility, and you must be vigilant.

Every word, thought, and action produces seeds for good or bad. Therefore, you must guard your heart (Proverbs 4:23) and remain faith-focused.

Below are five practical steps to put your faith in action daily:

1. Write down what you are believing God for.
2. Find supporting scriptures.
3. Confess the scriptures daily.
4. Don't let doubt, fear, or unbelief come out of your mouth.
5. Act on what God tells you to do.

My testimony started with conception. Long before trying to conceive, I began confessing and speaking to my body to do exactly what it was designed to do. Then, the first miracle happened. Despite using an IUD for the first five years of marriage and wrecking my hormones and immune system, I conceived the first month we tried. It was God and His Word! I was in no condition to get pregnant. Doctors said, "You need to get a stronger immune system first," but my husband and I felt it was the right time. I had blood work done with a natural doctor, and was told I had very low white and red blood cells. But we acted on what we felt, and knew it was the perfect time for us to have a baby.

After conceiving, I moved my confessions from conception to having an amazing pregnancy and the baby's development. At the twenty-week ultrasound scan, I remember being so overwhelmed by the goodness of God. I went in thinking they would tell me the gender, but I didn't realize they would tell me my baby had ten fingers, ten toes, and a four-chamber heart that had developed perfectly. Our baby was perfect in every way. Everything I had confessed was manifesting in this precious gift God had given us.

I was having an amazing pregnancy with no morning sickness, no pain, and no discomfort. I was active and healthy. I had some heartburn, but nothing major until thirty-seven weeks, when I tested positive for Group B Streptococcus (GBS), which is a bacteria that can be passed to your baby. This was the only issue we had the entire pregnancy. However, my faith did not waiver. I researched it in the natural to understand what it was. They recommended I take antibiotics during labor, but my faith was not in that place. Thankfully, I was at a great birth center, and they supported my decision to not take the antibiotics. I spoke to my body to come in line with God's Word for the remaining weeks of pregnancy. I *knew* it was impossible for GBS to be in my body because of what Jesus had done for me.

At thirty-nine weeks, I woke up and felt different, but I just thought, *Well, I am getting closer to the end of pregnancy*, and thought nothing of it. My mom was two weeks late with my sister, brother, and myself, so I expected to be two weeks late as well. But God knows when babies are conceived and when they need to be born. I know people have complications and need to deliver their babies early, but trust God and your body. They will come forth at the right time. One of the best things I've heard is you don't have a "due date," you have a due month. Add two weeks before and after your due date, and your baby will come within that time frame. Physically, I was not prepared. Mentally and spiritually, I was prepared, but I didn't have any bags packed or a place for the baby to sleep. I thought, *This baby is going to come in one to three weeks*, so I have time. I was wrong.

I started having contractions around noon. Later that day, my husband attended his best friend's bachelor party, and my mother-in-love, Veronique, and a friend came over to hang out. The contractions persisted and grew closer together. Veronique said, "I think we need to call Tim." I said, "Oh no, I will be okay. I'm a week early. There is no way this baby is coming today." She insisted on making me a bag to take to the birth center. She would ask where items were, and I tried telling her through the contractions. My husband saw everyone running to get stuff together on our security camera and came home and said, "Let's go." Of course, I said, "No. I don't want to get there and be two centimeters. I'm not going."

He called the doula and midwife, and they said, "Oh, this is probably early labor going into active labor. Take a bath and try to get some rest." I had lost my mucus plug and thrown up. At this point, I knew the baby would come in twenty-four hours, but I was still in denial. I thought, *Surely the contractions will stop, and I will get a good night's rest*. My husband insisted we go, but I assured him I just needed to rest. I took a bath to relax myself, and when I got out, my husband put a towel down on our bed and held my hand. My contractions grew stronger and more consistent, and my husband knew something was about to happen. Suddenly, my water broke, and it was like a water balloon bursting. He knew we needed to leave right away. I finally realized this was *actually* happening. I had not told anyone else what was going on. The only thing I could say was, "Oh my God, Oh my God, Oh my God. I need to call my mom."

I was getting clean pants and my husband, who is always calm, was telling me to get in the car. "I'm thirsty," I told him. I just wanted to get some water. He said, "Get in the car now!" I wondered why he was being so pushy. We headed to the birth center, and he let them know we were on the way. My husband texted my family saying, "water broke," which was a huge shock for them since they didn't know anything was going on. Statistically, I knew labor could stall on the drive to a medical facility, so I focused on staying in the labor zone. I put my head in my arm, occasionally looking up to give my husband directions. This annoyed my mom-in-love greatly. She thought, *This woman is in labor, and my son doesn't know where to go*, which makes me laugh now. It was about a forty-minute drive to the birth center. When we arrived, I looked at the door and said to myself, "I am not getting out of this car until someone comes to get me." Why? Who knows. When in labor, they say you go to "labor land." I don't know exactly where that is, but I can tell you, I was there.

The midwife helped me out of the car and walked me to my room. I had a big contraction, but she still thought I wasn't that far along and that we had a long night ahead of us. Most first-time moms don't have their babies early. If they do, labor is much longer than the eleven hours mine had been going. She checked me, and to everyone's surprise, except my husband's, I was 10 centimeters, 100 percent effaced, and the baby was at station two. This meant my daughter's head was coming out. Zero is at your pelvis, and once you get to station five, the baby is out. So we were almost there!

From previous conversations, the midwife knew I wanted a water birth, and told me I could get in the tub. As I walked to the tub, I said, "I don't know how to do this." She said, "What? Get in the tub?" I replied, "No, birth a baby." I got settled and into a good position, and they told me they wanted ten good pushes. They wanted me to take my time and not rush the delivery. I counted each push and could feel our baby coming down. My husband, who was not interested in learning anything about birth beforehand, was the most amazing partner for my labor. His job for this birth was to make an anointed playlist. He also placed cool cloths on my neck and head and gave me sips of water. For someone who was so disinterested in the process beforehand, I was shocked at how perfect and attentive he was during the entire labor.

I gave a good push, and I felt our daughter go down and then come back up. I felt discouraged. She was so close, and I felt like I lost some of the progress I made. The midwives assured me she was going to come and that I needed two more good pushes. On the tenth push, after about forty-five minutes of pushing, our daughter Eva Ann was born at 12:44 a.m. I had about twelve total hours of labor, and I was thrilled! Most first-time labors can last twenty-four hours or even go on for days.

The best part was the midwives telling me that even though I was GBS positive, because Eva came so quickly (and I was ready to push when I arrived) and was in the amniotic sac until the very end of my labor, when my water broke, they couldn't have administered the antibiotics even if I wanted them. As I held Eva, I knew she was God-given and perfect in every way.

It was important to share this testimony, so you understand where I was physically, mentally, and spiritually. Also, for you to realize that if you get a hold of God's Word, act on it in faith, and protect it, you can have what you are believing for. And that goes for anyone! For me, it was a supernatural childbirth, but what is it for you? What do you need? What do you want? What are you believing for? Are you contending for anything? What is God speaking to you to do or believe Him for? Maybe it's a husband, a new car, or a better job. Perhaps you need your ministry to go to the next level. Or maybe you need a miracle in your body.

> *Then Peter opened his mouth, and said, Of a truth I perceive that God is no respecter of persons:*
>
> Acts 10:34 KJV

This is more than encouraging your faith for conception or childbirth. This is for every area you are believing God for something. Spiritually, I needed to know what was available to me, but also what needed to happen in the natural. Some people get so built up in one area only, leaving out other areas of importance. We must remember that we live in a natural world with God's supernatural power made available to us. But this power only works if *you* work it! Remember, faith takes action. Faith *works* God's Word.

I consistently spoke to every part of my body, telling it to work and be perfectly aligned with God's Word. During my pregnancy, I told my sister, "I'm going to have a supernatural childbirth." I told her my friend Jacky had a supernatural childbirth and she said, "Well, she's Spanish, and Spanish ladies always have their babies quickly." As much as I love my sister, I stopped talking to her about what I believed for. I needed to talk to people who would join their faith with me. Even if it meant me only telling God what I was believing for.

Thankfully, my husband and I were in 100 percent agreement for a supernatural childbirth at a birth center. Unfortunately, I think a lot of people go wrong because they are not in agreement with their spouse.

> *Again I say to you, if two of you agree on earth about anything they ask, it will be done for them by my Father in heaven.*
>
> MATTHEW 18:19 ESV

If you are married, you need to be in agreement with your spouse. When you have a baby, it's not just *your* baby. The child belongs to both of you, and you must discuss how you are going to care for them. This includes knowing what procedures you'll allow the hospital to perform on the baby, and understanding what's necessary and unnecessary. And that goes for you personally. You cannot just let medical professionals do what *they* usually do, what *they* want to do, or even what *they* "think" is best.

 It is your job to educate yourself, and then ask God what to do in certain situations. Rest assured, He will lead and guide you.

We were very busy with work, which tended to be stressful at times. My husband talked to an amazing pastor at our church who told him, "Your kids are called and graced to do whatever you are called and graced to do. Kids are a blessing to your life, business, and ministry. They are not a hindrance." We didn't have kids earlier in marriage because we honestly didn't see how we could fit them in. I had friends with good intentions say, "When a girl wants to get pregnant, she can." But I wanted my husband's agreement on the timing because this decision affected both of our lives. Honestly, I don't think if I did something to have an "oops," my outcome would have been the same.

It's very easy to listen to others and take their advice. It may even be great, logical, and sound, but what is God speaking to you about? What is His best for you? During this pregnancy, my mom and sister were nurses. It would have been easy for me to take their advice, which was to have a hospital delivery. I actually began with midwives at a hospital, but I didn't feel that was the right place for me. My husband didn't either. If I was in the hospital, I might have had a different story with a different outcome. I don't know. Praise God I don't have to know, because I was willing to walk on His Word when He said, "Come, there is a better way." I had to listen and *act* on what *He* told *me* to do.

The way I did it is not for everyone. Some people need to be in a hospital, and I recognize that. For myself, God was calling me up higher in Him, and to a higher level of faith. He used childbirth to challenge me to grow! Not only did I grow in this area, but I grew in every area of my life. I want to leave you with this thought:

> *They go from strength to strength [increasing in victorious power]; each of them appears before God in Zion.*

> PSALM 84:7 AMPC

We should be increasing in victorious power! In order to do so, we must increase in the One Who gives us this power—God Almighty! When He calls us to act, we must obey.

Maybe believing God to have a baby outside of a hospital and without an epidural, seems like a silly way to go from strength to strength. But this was how He challenged me to go up higher and grow in Him. It was a walk of faith for me each step of the way. So where is He calling *you*? And will you carefully listen and fearlessly obey?

CHAPTER TWO

REPETITION REAPS RESULTS

Kelly's Story

What and who you listen to matters. What you allow yourself to consume is what you will become and emulate. Most have heard Romans 10:17 KJV which states:

> *So then faith cometh by hearing, and hearing by the word of God.*
>
> ROMANS 10:17 KJV

If you are around people who speak faith, you will speak faith. Likewise, if you fill your life with people who speak doubt and negativity, that's what will come out of you.

We are blessed to have some of the best pastors in the world, Drs. Rodney and Adonica Howard-Browne. If you don't know them, they are the founders of Revival Ministries International, The River Church at Tampa Bay, and River University in Tampa, Florida. In December 1987, Drs.

Rodney and Adonica, along with their three children, Kirsten, Kelly, and Kenneth, moved from their native land, South Africa, to the United States as missionaries sent by God. Upon arriving in America, they traveled across the nation in their Astro van, holding two meetings a day, six days a week, and forty-six weeks of the year, for fourteen years! Then God called them to start a church, and on December 1, 1996, they held their first service in the historic USF Sun Dome, with 575 people!

Throughout the years, hundreds of thousands of people have traveled from around the world for life-changing encounters with God, and their ministry continues to grow. At the time of writing this book, Drs. Rodney and Adonica have carried the Gospel to ninety-six countries, meeting the spiritual and physical needs of the domestic and international communities they faithfully serve.

Their second-born daughter, Kelly, was born with an incurable lung disease called Cystic Fibrosis. After many years of believing God for healing, seeing many miracles, and facing many battles, on Christmas morning 2002, at the young age of eighteen, Kelly breathed her last breath and went home to be with Jesus. They placed Kelly into the arms of her Lord and Savior and said, "We aren't going to let the devil take her from us. Today, we give You, the Lord, our best gift." Then they vowed, "The devil would pay for what he had done to their family." Secondly, they vowed "To do everything in their power, with the help of the Lord, to win 100 million souls to Jesus and to put $1 Billion into world missions and the harvest of souls." Dr. Rodney is also raising up 300 multimillionaires to fund the end-time harvest through the ministry's Kingdom Business Fellowship.

VICTORIOUS IN BATTLE

I don't know about you, but if I just lost my eighteen-year-old daughter, I am not sure that would have been my reaction. They handled that situation with such dignity, strength, and grace. I have heard this story many times, and what stands out the most is their reverence and love for the Lord through the toughest moments life could bring. Since Kelly went to Heaven on Christmas morning, her story is usually told on or around Christmas. How do you lose your daughter on Christmas Day and still have joy? I can tell you it's possible, because I have seen my pastors walk it out firsthand. There is no anger or bitterness. There is no resentment. Of course, they would love to have their daughter here, but she is dancing on streets of gold. One of the associate pastors had a vision of Kelly in Heaven, looking over the banisters of Heaven and seeing her earthly body saying, "Yuck, I hate that thing." Once you experience His glory, you don't want anything this world has to offer. Even though this meant leaving her family behind.

Kelly's story reminds me of Abraham and Isaac in Genesis:

After these events, God tested and proved Abraham and said to him, Abraham! And he said, Here I am. [God] said, Take now your son, your only son Isaac, whom you love, and go to the region of Moriah; and offer him there as a burnt offering upon one of the mountains of which I will tell you. So Abraham rose early in the morning, saddled his donkey, and took two of his young men with him and his son Isaac; and he split the wood for the burnt offering, and then began the trip to the place of which God had told him. On the third day Abraham looked up and saw the place in the distance. And Abraham said to his servants, Settle down and stay here with the donkey, and I and the young man will go yonder and worship and come again to you. Then Abraham took the wood for the burnt offering and laid it on [the shoulders of] Isaac his son, and he took the fire (the firepot) in his own hand, and a knife; and the two of them went on together. And Isaac said to Abraham, My father! And he said, Here I am, my son. [Isaac] said, See, here are the fire and the wood, but where is the lamb for the burnt sacrifice? Abraham said, My son, God Himself will provide a lamb for the burnt offering. So the two went on together. When they came to the place of which God had told him, Abraham built an altar there; then he laid the wood in order and bound Isaac his son and laid him on the altar on the wood. [Matthew 10:37] And Abraham stretched forth his hand and took hold of the knife to slay his son. [Heb. 11:17-19.] But the Angel of the Lord called to him from heaven and said, Abraham, Abraham! He answered, Here I am. And He said, Do not lay your hand on the lad or do anything to him; for now I know that you fear and revere God, since you have not held back from Me or begrudged giving Me your son, your only son. Then Abraham looked up and glanced around, and behold, behind him was a ram caught in a thicket by his horns. And Abraham went and took the ram and offered it up for a burnt offering and an ascending sacrifice instead of his son! So Abraham called the name of that place The Lord Will Provide. And it is said to this day, On the mount of the Lord it will be provided. The Angel of the Lord called to Abraham from heaven a second time And said, I have sworn by Myself, says the Lord, that since you have done this and have not withheld [from Me] or begrudged [giving Me] your son, your only son, In blessing I will bless you and in multiplying I will multiply your descendants like the stars of the heavens and like the sand on the seashore. And your Seed (Heir) will possess the gate of His enemies, [Heb. 6:13, 14; 11:12] And in your Seed [Christ] shall all the nations of the earth be blessed and [by Him] bless themselves, because you have heard and obeyed My voice.

GENESIS 22:1-18 AMPC

Abram heard God's instructions, and he acted. That action is what gives us access to the covenant we have today. My pastors lost their daughter, but ultimately that day, an altar was built before the Lord. That day, they gave their best gift. Many people are not willing to make the sacrifice they made, which is why they have what most people do not have. Their example of overcoming such a tough situation has greatly impacted my life and so many others.

It is easy to come to church and think, *Oh, I've heard this before*, *I know this story or testimony the pastor is telling*, or *I know this scripture and, I can quote it in every version*. That's great. But if you aren't the pastor, or the pastor isn't calling you up to share, you should probably listen to what they have to say. I have heard the same stories for over seventeen years now. And every time I come to church, I ask God to reveal more of Himself to me, and for deeper revelation. I ask Him to show me what I am missing or don't know. I love the way I Corinthians 1:25 puts it:

[This is] because the foolish thing [that has its source in] God is wiser than men, and the weak thing [that springs] from God is stronger than men.

I Corinthians 1:25 AMPC

No matter what I know, it's nothing compared to what God knows and Who He is. No matter what I have learned, I can always learn more. I am thirty-five years old now and still learning. I have been in church since I was in my mother's womb. As a teen, I was challenged to read the Bible cover to cover each year, which I have done many times and still endeavor to do today. I am here to testify to you, the more you read His Word, the more you want it, the more you crave it, and the more you need it. I still read the Word and get fresh revelations daily. When I go to church, even if I have heard what the pastor is saying, I say to myself, "This is exactly what I needed to hear today." It's important to adjust our attitude and mindset. We must ask God to show us the men and women of God we are to receive from.

Your pastor is put in their office by God. They are there as a shepherd to the flock. If I'm in the flock, I'm there to listen and learn from my shepherd. Saying, "*I've heard this before,*" will reap nothing in your life. And I want you to reap all that God has for you, and continue to grow. When you are under a man or woman of God you respect, it becomes easy to receive from them, regardless of how many times you have heard a message. If it wasn't for our pastor telling Kelly's story repeatedly, I'll be honest, I do not know where I would be.

As I have sat under this ministry, I have grown in faith, learned, and continue to learn. Below are seven foundational truths and absolutes of the Word that I learned from my pastors.

 Nothing in the Word changes. When you look at the Word as an absolute, and not a suggestion, you operate at a different level.

1. Faith comes by hearing and hearing the Word of God.

So then faith cometh by hearing, and hearing by the word of God.

ROMANS 10:17 KJV

2. He honors His Word above His very Name.

I will worship toward Your holy temple and praise Your name for Your loving-kindness and for Your truth and faithfulness; for You have exalted above all else Your name and Your word and You have magnified Your word above all Your name!

PSALM 138:2 AMPC

3. He doesn't change. He is the same yesterday, today, and forever.

For I am the Lord, I do not change; that is why you, O sons of Jacob, are not consumed.

MALACHI 3:6 AMPC

In the beginning was the Word, and the Word was with God, and the Word was God.

JOHN 1:1 KJV

Jesus Christ the same yesterday, and today, and forever.

HEBREWS 13:8 KJV

4. His Word is the living Word of God. It's active and alive.

For the Word that God speaks is alive and full of power [making it active, operative, energizing, and effective]; it is sharper than any two-edged sword, penetrating to the dividing line of the breath of life (soul) and [the immortal] spirit, and of joints and marrow [of the deepest parts of our nature], exposing and sifting and analyzing and judging the very thoughts and purposes of the heart.

HEBREWS 4:12 AMPC

5. He will remain.

They will perish, but You remain and continue permanently; they will all grow old and wear out like a garment.

HEBREWS 1:11 AMPC

I am the Alpha and the Omega, the First and the Last (the Before all and the End of all) [Isa. 44:6; 48:12]

REVELATION 22:13 AMPC
(SCRIPTURE REFERENCE ADDED)

6. Every Scripture is God-breathed.

Every Scripture is God-breathed (given by His inspiration) and profitable for instruction, for reproof and conviction of sin, for correction of error and discipline in obedience, [and] for training in righteousness (in holy living, in conformity to God's will in thought, purpose, and action), So that the man of God may be complete and proficient, well fitted and thoroughly equipped for every good work.

2 TIMOTHY 3:16 AMPC

7. The joy of the Lord is your strength.

Then [Ezra] told them, Go your way, eat the fat, drink the sweet drink, and send portions to him for whom nothing is prepared; for this day is holy to our Lord. And be not grieved and depressed, for the joy of the Lord is your strength and stronghold.

NEHEMIAH 8:10 AMPC

This is why the Word works. Your situation is not greater than the Word. If Jesus was tempted by the devil with the Word, it's foolish to think the devil won't come to us with the

Word or temptations. Every battle is an opportunity to do what God says, or give into what our natural minds think or want. The Word must be the final answer. It is our absolute!

CHAPTER THREE

THE ATTACK

The Miscarriage Story

In the summer of 2017, I got pregnant with our second child. I was still nursing our daughter Eva, and even though my periods were a little bit irregular, nothing was considered abnormal. We told a few close friends and family members that we were pregnant. My sister and I were two years apart, and I really wanted our kids to be two years apart as well. I went in for my first few appointments and saw our growing baby. I was so excited!

We were living in Utah for the summer for work, and we were heading home at the end of August. I flew home a few days earlier than Tim, with our daughter Eva. Everything seemed fine, and I felt totally normal. Once Tim got home, we went to the appointment to hear the baby's heartbeat. At this appointment, they couldn't find the heartbeat, however, this was not abnormal. I was eleven weeks and a few days pregnant. They asked me to come back the following day for an ultrasound. We prayed and agreed that our baby was fine and would be perfect and whole. That evening, I started having some very faint bleeding. Again, it was not totally abnormal for this stage of pregnancy. It was not great news, but we still believed our baby would be born without any complications. We knew there were various reasons these things could happen, and we knew God was on our side. We got something to eat and spent time playing outside with our daughter.

Once back inside, I was in the laundry room when I felt a gush of water come out. At that moment, I knew I was going to miscarry our baby, and that there was no way the baby could make it. I ran to the bathroom and called my husband. I told him what was happening. What happened next would change the course of our lives forever! For the first time in our married lives, we were facing a *real* fight. At that moment, we had a vital decision to make. How would we handle this situation? What would our reaction be? Fear, Anger, Despair?

Often, you don't realize what is in you until you are put in a high-pressure situation. What came out of us was beautiful and glorious. It was praise! We thanked God for the eleven weeks and four days He entrusted our baby to us.

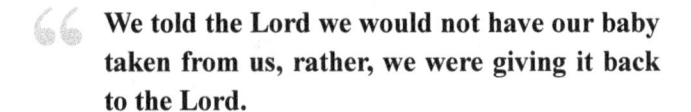

> **We told the Lord we would not have our baby taken from us, rather, we were giving it back to the Lord.**

We were giving Him our best gift, and we praised and worshiped the Lord. That's what we were taught to do, and that is what was in us. When we were pressed, squeezed, and attacked, praise is what came out. The example from our pastors, as well as others like Evangelists Jonathan and

Adalis Shuttlesworth, became a reality for my husband and I in the moment we needed it most. For over a year, after hearing them teach on the power of praise, we got up daily, praising God with all our might. Little did I know, those seeds of praise would carry us through the darkest time. We praised when we felt like it, we praised when we didn't. We praised when we had victories, we praised when we faced battles. No matter what, we praised God in everything we did. On the good days and the bad days, we conditioned ourselves that the first thing we would do is praise the Lord. So, in what should have been one of our worst moments, we had peace in our hearts and praise in our mouths.

We didn't know that losing the baby was just the beginning of the devil's attack that night. After the initial rush, we called the midwives and told them what happened. It was the same midwife who delivered Eva who answered. I was incredibly grateful for her, she was so sweet and kind. She told me I should be prepared to lose a lot of blood and when to seek medical attention if necessary. 10 p.m. came and went, 11 p.m., 12 a.m. rolled around, and at about 2 a.m., we realized something might be wrong. Every hour, I lost large amounts of blood. Somewhere in the early hours of the morning, I passed the baby. I picked my baby up from the floor and flushed it down the toilet. I didn't know what else to do.

At this point, I thought, *I passed the baby and now, the blood will slow down*, but it didn't. The bathroom looked like a scene from a horror film. My husband was sitting on the floor and felt we needed to head to the hospital. Around 4 a.m., we left our home with our daughter sleeping in the back seat. Up until this point, I felt *ok* under the circumstances.

We arrived at the emergency room, and as I walked inside to check in, I suddenly felt different, and not in a good way. I said to the lady at the registration desk, "I am having a miscarriage, and I need someone to help me." She replied, "There is a bathroom over there." I said, "Ma'am, I am losing a lot of blood and I need help." I started to pass out. At that exact moment, my husband walked in and caught me right as I fell. He laid me on the ground as the doctors and nurses rushed over to me. After blacking out for a few seconds, I woke up to my daughter screaming, my husband praying, and the medical staff in a panic. I felt like I was asleep and had just woken up. They put me in a wheelchair and rushed me over to check my vitals. Their faces turned white, and they said they needed a room for me right away. They were racing down the hallway when I passed out again. This time, I was fully aware of what was happening...I was dying.

Everything felt like a scene from a movie. It was like I saw myself being rushed down the hall and white lights all around. Not hospital lights, but the light of the glory of Heaven. I thought, *If I die, I will leave my husband a widower and my daughter without a mother. That will not be their story.* The only thing I could muster from my spirit was, "I will live and not die. I will live and not die!" My spirit returned to my body as we arrived at the room. Doctors started working on me, sticking me with God only knows what, and hooking me up to all the machines. They retook my vitals and were puzzled. My vitals were returning to normal. They couldn't understand how, only minutes before, a lifeless person on the floor was suddenly alive and back to normal.

Although I was stable, I was still losing a lot of blood. The ER doctor was a kind and sympathetic man, and I am very grateful for him. He did the best he could without being an

OBGYN. Upon a pelvic examination, he discovered a piece of the placenta was stuck. Every time my uterus tried to clamp down, it couldn't because of the obstruction causing blood loss. My body was shaking and very tense. I remembered something from Jackie Mize's book, *Supernatural Childbirth*, that I used a lot during my pregnancy, labor, and delivery. She always said, "Be calm, at peace, and relaxed." I spoke to my body, saying, "Body, you get in line with the Word of God. You be calm, at peace, and relaxed. Just like my body was designed to carry and bring forth a baby, it's designed to bring forth this placenta too."

Tim turned on *By His Stripes*, a CD with healing scriptures by Dr. Rodney Howard-Browne. If you are battling anything in your body, I highly recommend you play that nonstop. The ER doctor explained he was unable to remove the obstruction and needed to get it out. He said he would contact the on-call OBGYNs for assistance, but if they couldn't help, he would explain more invasive options for treatment. Everyone left the room, and Tim and I prayed and believed God for the least invasive procedure possible to get the desired results. We spoke to my body, thanking God for the miracle we already had, and asking Him to complete the work and fix this situation.

The OBGYNs came in with their snarky attitudes, making me feel like I had a miscarriage because I used midwives for my prenatal care. I put that aside and spoke to my body to be calm, at peace, relaxed, and aligned with God's Word. And it did just that! They successfully removed the piece of placenta, which came with more snide commentary. They finished by telling me I needed follow-up care, questioning *if a midwife was qualified* to provide it. I forgave them because they only knew what they were taught. I am thankful they helped me. However, I am grateful they were not my primary providers. The ER doctor returned and kept me for monitoring before releasing me a few hours later.

We planned to make our big announcement the following week. Instead, we had to tell our friends and family what happened that night, and that we would meet our precious baby in Heaven. I'll be honest, I wonder what our baby looks like. I am pretty sure it's a little girl. Regardless, I know our baby is waiting for us, and I look forward to meeting the fifth member of our family on that glorious day.

That night, we saw the importance of hearing Kelly's story and understood the importance of praise. Those truths saved us in our darkest hour. We were never mad or blamed God. We kept our hearts pure before the Lord, and watched Him turn our tragedy into triumph.

Remember, the devil doesn't have any new tricks. He tries the same attacks repeatedly, and we must decide not to fall for them. I call it the "3 D's".

The devil wants to:

1. Discourage you
2. Distract you
3. Deceive you

If anything happens in your life that causes one of the "3 D's," know it's the devil, and he is up to the same scheming he's done since the beginning of time. What did he do to Eve? He deceived her! He is the master of deception. Just look at the beginning in Genesis:

Now the serpent was more subtle and crafty than any living creature of the field which the Lord God had made. And he [Satan] said to the woman, Can it really be that God has said, You shall not eat from every tree of the garden? [Rev. 12:9-11.] And the woman said to the serpent, We may eat the fruit from the trees of the garden, Except the fruit from the tree which is in the middle of the garden. God has said, You shall not eat of it, neither shall you touch it, lest you die. But the serpent said to the woman, You shall not surely die, [II Cor. 11:3.] For God knows that in the day you eat of it your eyes will be opened, and you will be like God, knowing the difference between good and evil and blessing and calamity. And when the woman saw that the tree was good (suitable, pleasant) for food and that it was delightful to look at, and a tree to be desired in order to make one wise, she took of its fruit and ate; and she gave some also to her husband, and he ate. Then the eyes of them both were opened, and they knew that they were naked; and they sewed fig leaves together and made themselves apronlike girdles.

GENESIS 3:1-7 AMPC

The devil wants you to accept a life of less than what Jesus paid for you to have. Look at Cain. He was discouraged by his offering, which was not acceptable to the Lord. Let's look at Genesis 4:

And in the course of time Cain brought to the Lord an offering of the fruit of the ground. And Abel brought of the firstborn of his flock and of the fat portions. And the Lord had respect and regard for Abel and for his offering, [Heb. 11:4.] But for Cain and his offering He had no respect or regard. So Cain was exceedingly angry and indignant, and he looked sad and depressed. And the Lord said to Cain, Why are you angry? And why do you look sad and depressed and dejected? If you do well, will you not be accepted? And if you do not do well, sin crouches at your door; its desire is for you, but you must master it. And Cain said to his brother, Let us go out to the field. And when they were in the field, Cain rose up against Abel his brother and killed him. [I John 3:12.] And the Lord said to Cain, Where is Abel your brother? And he said, I do not know. Am I my brother's keeper? And [the Lord] said, What have you done? The voice of your brother's blood is crying to Me from the ground. And now you are cursed by reason of the earth, which has opened its mouth to receive your brother's [shed] blood from your hand.

GENESIS 4:3-11 AMPC
(SCRIPTURE REFERENCE ADDED)

Finally, we can see where everyone was deceived when building the Tower of Babel in Genesis.

And the whole earth was of one language and of one accent and mode of expression. And as they journeyed eastward, they found a plain (valley) in the land of Shinar, and they settled and dwelt there. And they said one to another, Come, let us make bricks and burn them thoroughly. So they had brick for stone, and slime (bitumen) for mortar. And they said, Come, let us build us a city and a tower whose top reaches into the sky, and let us make a name for ourselves, lest we be scattered over the whole earth. And the Lord came down to see the city and the tower which the sons of men had built. And the Lord said, Behold, they are one people and they have all one language; and this is only the beginning of what they will do, and now nothing they have imagined they can do will be impossible for them. Come, let Us go down and there confound (mix up, confuse) their language, that they may not understand one another's speech.

GENESIS 11:1-7

The idea to build the Tower of Babel didn't come from the Lord, so where do you think it came from? Anything in life is either from God or somewhere else. Anything that is not God's best, you can assume is from the devil. People settle for just *enough* or just *okay*, but that is *not* God's best. If you go through anything in life, and it's not from God, just know it's from the enemy. John 8 paints a clear picture:

For you are the children of your father the devil, and you love to do the evil things he does. He was a murderer from the beginning. He has always hated the truth, because there is no truth in him. When he lies, it is consistent with his character; for he is a liar and the father of lies.

JOHN 8:44 NLT

The devil is the father of lies. If something in your life discourages, distracts, or deceives you, it's from the devil. It's plain and simple. Attacks are not from God. Romans 14:17 tells us what the Kingdom of God established is about:

For the kingdom of God is not meat and drink; but righteousness, and peace, and joy in the Holy Ghost.

ROMAN 14:7 KJV

If it's not righteousness, peace, and joy, it's probably the devil.

Say This Now:

I am overcoming. I am overcoming all attacks from the enemy. God does not want me to be discouraged, distracted, deceived, or defeated. He desires for me to have righteousness, peace, and joy. He desires for me to be strong in the Lord and the power of His might. No matter what comes, I am strong and getting stronger, in Jesus' Name!

CHAPTER FOUR

THE BATTLE

Keeping the Joy

The most surprising things can happen in the midst of the greatest battle. We played *By His Stripes* the entire time in the hospital, and around 8 a.m., we were heading home. All of a sudden, a song came on that marked us—*Give Thanks*, written by Henry Smith and sung by Eddie James. You may have heard it…

> Give thanks with a grateful heart
> Give thanks to the Holy One
> Give thanks because He's given
> Jesus Christ, His Son
>
> Give thanks with a grateful heart
> Give thanks to the Holy One
> Give thanks because He's given
> Jesus Christ, His Son
>
> And now let the weak say, I am strong

Let the poor say, I am rich
Because of what the Lord has done for us

And now let the weak say, I am strong
Let the poor say, I am rich
Because of what the Lord has done for us

Give thanks
Give Him thanks
Give thanks
Give Him thanks

I don't think I had ever heard of Eddie James up until that moment. If you have never heard that song, I encourage you to listen to it. In the song, he exhorts the people listening. He says, "Just begin to praise the Lord. If you are in the delivery room, praise Him. If you are at work, praise Him. If you are in the car, praise Him. I don't care who is watching, I know Who's worthy." Man, that hit me so hard. And at that moment, the peace of God flooded my husband and I. His joy came, and we started laughing. How do you go from losing a baby and almost dying, to praising the Lord with joy and gladness in a few hours? Only the Lord could do it. A few moments with the Lord can do what no one else could do for you in years.

Nothing on this Earth could've helped me how Jesus did. No psychologist could have given me that peace. My husband and I never look back on that moment as victims, but as victorious. I never want someone to hear this story and feel sorry for us. I want people to hear it and think about God's goodness!

> **I don't want people to hug me and feel how much I've suffered. I hope they hug me and feel how victorious I am.**

During this time, I found scriptures to stand on that I want to share. Although I had this amazing moment of victory in the car, the devil does what he does best. He wants to deceive, discourage, and distract you. He tried discouraging me with lies and guilt to make me believe what happened was my fault, and had I done something different or better, this never would have happened. So, every time he came, I had the sword (which is the Word) ready to defeat him.

First, I settled something once and for all—God is good. The end! There is nothing else to it. God didn't want "another rose for His garden." He didn't send this as a test for us to see what we would do. This was not His will or His best for my life. I encourage you to settle this for yourself when facing challenges. How do you settle it, you ask? You go with what the Word says. The Word is final and absolute. It never fails, and it never changes. Your situation is not above and doesn't change the Word.

The Word will work for every situation, every time. Do you believe it? Not, do you *think* about it, but do you *know* it? Do you know it in your head, in your heart, and in spirit? You need to know it every way you look at it. If you know it in one area and not in another, you will waiver and can be defeated. If you want to win victoriously in battle, the Word must be your absolute every time. There can be no other option.

These were my three absolutes when it came to my victory:

1. The devil comes to steal, kill, and destroy. God gives life and life abundantly.

> *The thief comes only in order to steal and kill and destroy. I came that they may have and enjoy life, and have it in abundance (to the full, till it overflows)*

> JOHN 10:10 AMPC

Whose fingerprints does your situation have? God's or the devil's? If it's life and life abundantly overflowing, it's God! If it is pain, sorrow, destruction, and death…you guessed it. That's the devil, every time. You must settle that. I've seen people suffer loss and get mad at God, but they are mad at the wrong one. The devil wants you mad at God, but never give him the satisfaction of giving into his plan.

2. God lives in our praise.

> *But thou art holy, O thou that inhabitest the praises of Israel*

> PSALM 22:3 KJV

Inhabits - Yashab yaw-shab Hebrew
1. (*v. t.*) To live or dwell in; to occupy, as a place of settled residence; as wild beasts inhabit the forest; men inhabit cities and houses.
2. (*v. i.*) To have residence in a place; to dwell; to live; to abide.

This verse tells us God inhabits the praise of Israel, His people. It doesn't say God inhabits our pain, sorrow, or our feelings. If I want God with me, I need to praise Him. It doesn't say He will inhabit our praises when we feel like praising Him, and this is a major key. Every time the devil tried lying to me, I praised. I would put on *Give Thanks* by Eddie James and praise the Lord repeatedly. Sometimes, I would do it with tears streaming down my face, but I praised Him anyway. My situation or circumstance didn't matter, and yours don't either.

I don't mean that insincerely, but if you want victory, you must get to a place of victory. Victory will not come by feeling sorry for yourself or defeated. Victory will not come if you are blaming God. If you don't want to stay where you are, you have to praise Him. I know people have been through far worse than what I went through. If you have, I am sorry. But I want you to be a victor more than I want you to be a victim. There is power in your praise!

God resides in our praise. The more I need Him, the more I need to praise Him. In life, we often want shortcuts or cheat codes, and this is the ultimate one. I dare you to genuinely praise God every day for ten minutes a day for a month, and tell me you are not in a better place than you were thirty-days ago. I love Psalm 34:1, which says:

> *I will bless the LORD at all times; His praise shall continually be in my mouth.*
>
> PSALM 34:1 AMPC

If you want to know how much you can or should praise Him, *continually* is sufficient according to His Word.

3. The Joy of the Lord is your strength.

> *Then [Ezra] told them, Go your way, eat the fat, drink the sweet drink, and send portions to him for whom nothing is prepared; for this day is holy to our Lord. And be not grieved and depressed, for the joy of the Lord is your strength and stronghold.*
>
> Nehemiah 8:10 AMPC

It might sound cliché, but it's the Word. So don't allow yourself to be grieved or depressed. I could have given into grief, and I had every reason to. You might have every reason as well, but as Dr. Adonica says, "You might have a reason, but you don't have a right." I don't have a right to be depressed because the Lord said His joy is my strength. I see you coming out today and walking in victory.

> **I see victory rising on the inside of you. I see your situation changing!**

When you hear the Word, your faith grows. When your faith grows, you act on it. And when you act, things start to change. So get dressed, and do something that makes you feel nice. His joy gives you strength, so act in faith! His word promises joy:

> *For His anger is but for a moment, but His favor is for a lifetime or in His favor is life. Weeping may endure for a night, but joy comes in the morning.*
>
> Psalm 30:5 AMPC

Second Corinthians 4:17 tells us how to view every trouble:

For our present troubles are small and won't last very long. Yet they produce for us a glory that vastly outweighs them and will last forever!

2 CORINTHIANS 4:17 NLT

When you know the Lord promises joy and sees trouble as a small and temporary thing, you have to ask yourself, "How long can I stay down? How long will I continue to stay in a place of pain?" It's not God's will for you or anyone to stay there.

This brings us back to praise:

The Lord is my Strength and my [impenetrable] Shield; my heart trusts in, relies on, and confidently leans on Him, and I am helped; therefore my heart greatly rejoices, and with my song will I praise Him.

Psalm 28:7 AMPC

You must be strong to handle life, and joy and strength are found in the Lord. Mishandling a situation is evidence of a weakness in that area, lack of revelation, or both. Forgive yourself for what you didn't know. Forgive your parents and pastors for what they didn't teach you and go forth with this new knowledge and revelation.

I know I am not Joel Osteen. I am Simone. Life has thrown me some curveballs, and I had to grow up and be tough. You might say, "I'm not that tough," but "Yes, you *are*!" Do you know how I know you are strong? If you are saved and have Jesus in your heart, you are stronger than you realize.

> *I have told you these things, so that in Me you may have [perfect] peace and confidence. In the world you have tribulation and trials and distress and frustration; but be of good cheer [take courage; be confident, certain, undaunted]! For I have overcome the world. [I have deprived it of power to harm you and have conquered it for you.]*

JOHN 16:33 AMPC

If you are a saved, blood-washed, born-again believer, you can go forth boldly in Heaven's strength. The world offers trials, fear, worry, and weakness, but the Word says Jesus has *deprived the world of its power to harm you*. That's something to rejoice and be glad about!

As believers, we can choose to believe God's Word, or succumb to the world, denying the power of the Blood of Jesus. I pray that from this moment, that will be the easiest decision you ever make. May today be the day you draw the line in the sand and choose to be strong in the Lord and the power of His might. From today, you will believe and speak the Word, work the Word, and most importantly, act on the Word in faith!

Take the verses below, and fill your name in the blank:

"...The joy of the Lord is _____ strength and stronghold" (Nehemiah 8:10 AMP).

"The Lord is _____ strength and my [impenetrable] shield. _____ heart trusts with unwavering confidence] in Him, and I am helped; Therefore _____ heart greatly rejoices, And with my song I shall thank Him *and* praise Him" (Psalm 28:7 AMP).

"_____ will bless the LORD at all times; His praise shall continually be in _____ mouth" (Psalm 34:1 AMP).

"in every situation [no matter what the circumstances] _____ is thankful *and* continually gives thanks *to God*; for this is the will of God for you in Christ Jesus" (1 Thessalonians 5:18 AMP).

You can't say those scriptures and feel bad. You can't say them and not feel victory rise in you. The devil wants to keep you repeating his lies, but STOP! Don't give in, and don't do it! It would be better for you to say nothing. If someone asks how you're doing, say, "I am strong and getting stronger." You might not feel like it on day one, but the more you do and say it, it will become your reality. I encourage you to get a Bible with room to write notes. Take every scripture in the Bible pertaining to your situation and write your name in there. If it's in God's Word, it's available to you. If His Word says you can have joy and peace, put your name in there. If it says you are healed, that's for you! If it is good and made available to you, take it and make it yours!

> **Confess the Word with your name and watch the Word work.**

Some people like to be victims, but Jesus is our example. He defeated death, hell, and the grave. If He can do that, you can be victorious in every situation too, I promise. Understand, I am not saying you will never have another battle. Rather, you will handle it better than you did yesterday. God is unending, and we can never fully know Him. However, we can always grow more in Him, so choose to grow more today. In the words of my pastor, choose to "run towards the roar" and face every obstacle head-on with the Word.

The miscarriage and near-death experience wasn't a battle, it was an attack, and Jesus touched and restored me. However, the battle was in my mind. I had to choose the direction I'd go in. I cried, I grieved, and I let myself feel what I felt was necessary. Then I tightened up my combat boots, and as my husband says, "We kicked the devil in the face." Today, join me and make the devil regret he ever touched you or your family. Today, let's kick the devil in the face with praise, faith, and by acting on God's Word.

CHAPTER FIVE

THE VICTORY

How We Won

We definitely had the victory. Yes, we experienced loss, but ultimately, I was alive and counted that a win. I was also healthy and not having any further complications, but we had some immediate decisions to make. The most important one would tell Heaven and hell where we stood, what we believed, and what we would act upon.

We were scheduled to go to Finland, Italy, and Amsterdam to conduct Kingdom Business meetings. My husband and I believe part of our calling is funding the end-time harvest and lifting up the arms of men and women of God, seeing their visions come to pass. We know amazing people worldwide who are willing to forsake all and follow Jesus. They want to see their city and nations saved, and we want to see people link arms with them, ensuring the call is fulfilled.

We came home early Wednesday morning and needed to sleep. We were supposed to leave on Friday for our international flight. My husband and I discussed it, and we both felt this was an attack. Not only on me, but on our whole family. The devil wanted to know how we would react. He wanted to see if this would sideline us. Little did he know we would choose to rise to greatness. We decided we would not be pushed around. Being raised in Oklahoma, the best way to put it is, "We had to cowboy up." We had to get tough. A famous quote says, "When the going gets tough, the tough get going." This was one of those moments. We had to be tougher than any situation or circumstance. So we rested Wednesday, packed Thursday, and Friday, we headed to the airport.

I had to have blood work done, and my midwives cleared me for travel. They said if I passed any large blood clots, I needed to let them know right away. I felt a little weak, but that was expected. We were sleep deprived and had a few long days. As we were waiting at the gate, I ran to the bathroom before boarding. Of course, I passed a very large blood clot. I said, "Devil, I have already decided I am not going to let you push me around. I am getting on this plane, flying to my destination safely, and that's the end of this attack." I got on that plane and never looked back.

Before we got on the plane I was reminded of the sweet-smelling aroma of a sacrifice to God. Throughout the Word, sacrifices were either rejected like Cain's, or were a sweet-smelling aroma to God.

> *But I have all, and abound: I am full, having received of Epaphroditus the things which were sent from you, an odour of a sweet smell, a sacrifice acceptable, wellpleasing to God.*

PHILIPPIANS 4:18 KJV

VICTORIOUS IN BATTLE

For the entire month, we traveled, and my body was healing. I was reminded that how we handled the situation was precious in God's sight. But also, at that moment, we knew it would have been easy to stay home and rest. It would have been easy to let my body recover at home instead of traveling through Europe. But we knew what was in our spirits, so we went in the opposite direction of what the devil wanted us to do. And this is a vital key to living victoriously. You must wake up everyday and decide to go in the opposite direction of what the devil wants you to do. No matter how you feel in the moment, don't give in to what the devil wants.

When a woman has a baby, her body needs time to rest, recover, and heal. In the delivery process, the placenta leaves an open wound inside of the mother, and when it detaches from her uterus, she has to heal internally. Many don't realize this, but a woman must heal the same way after a miscarriage.

The doctors warned me to expect severe afterbirth pains and discomfort. When I told any doctor, nurse, or midwife that I experienced no pain or discomfort, they said, "Oh, you have a high pain tolerance." I don't think I do, but I know it was Jesus Who took all of my pain. He bore it all, paying the price for me to live healed and whole. He took away all of the physical, mental, and emotional pain. He did that for me, and will do that for you, whatever your battle is.

In Europe, we didn't skip a beat or slow down. We completed everything that needed to be done. Only our family and a few close friends knew what happened. No one around us knew what was going on. We were not going to let anything keep us from what we knew God had called us to do. We enjoyed our time, and even went to the Leaning Tower of Pisa at 2 a.m.

When God is with you, no one and nothing can stop you. When He quickens you, no sickness or attack can hold you back, unless you let it.

> **I decided I was strong, and acted upon it. I decided I was emotionally well, and my emotions followed.**

I decided no attack would hold us back, and it didn't. Did I feel it everyday? No. Did I always feel strong? No. Sometimes, I had to tell myself I was strong and that I could handle anything. I told myself what I was allowed to feel, and I let myself cry if I felt I needed to. However, I knew crying all day and laying in the bed wasn't going to help me, my husband, our daughter, or my walk with God. I filled myself with 1 Peter 5:6-10:

> *Therefore humble yourselves [demote, lower yourselves in your own estimation] under the mighty hand of God, that in due time He may exalt you, Casting the whole of your care [all your anxieties, all your worries, all your concerns, once and for all] on Him, for He cares for you affectionately and cares about you watchfully. [Ps. 55:22.] Be well balanced (temperate, sober of mind), be vigilant and cautious at all times; for that enemy of yours, the devil, roams around like a lion roaring [in fierce hunger], seeking someone to seize upon and devour. Withstand him; be firm in faith [against his onset–rooted, established, strong, immovable, and determined], knowing that the same (identical) sufferings are appointed to your brotherhood (the whole body of Christians) throughout the world. And after you have suffered a*

little while, the God of all grace [Who imparts all blessing and favor], Who has called you to His [own] eternal glory in Christ Jesus, will Himself complete and make you what you ought to be, establish and ground you securely, and strengthen, and settle you.

1 Peter 5:6-10 AMPC
(scripture reference added)

The enemy sought to devour me, and he seeks to devour you, but will you let him? Will you give in, or will you humble yourself as verse 6 says, and cast every concern on the Lord? It says He cares for you, but do you believe it? Do you know it? Is it deep in your spirit so that you're unwavering? You might think it's that Oklahoma "Cowgirl up" mentality, but trust me, it's so much more! He made us strong and mighty. When reading the Old Testament, I love phrases like, "Men of valor," or "Mighty men." I get excited, picturing the Israelite army full of real men who were strong, wise, witty, bold, and courageous. You don't kill a lion or a bear being weak. You kill them with boldness and unshakeable courage. I love reading about these men because that's how every believer should be—mighty with God's strength.

During this time, I meditated on Psalm 18—*I can run through a troop and leap over a wall*. I wrote out what God's characteristics enabled me to do. I didn't *feel* like I could leap over a wall, but if He said I could, I was determined to build myself up in the Word, so I always felt strong and ready to fight.

Sometimes, I've needed a word from the Lord, my family, or my husband to encourage me, but that's okay. King David also encouraged himself in the Lord:

David was greatly distressed, for the men spoke of stoning him because the souls of them all were bitterly grieved, each man for his sons and daughters. But David encouraged and strengthened himself in the Lord his God.

1 SAMUEL 30:6 AMPC

If David needed encouragement, it's okay for you or me to need encouragement. However, it's not okay to remain defeated, living in fear, anxiety, and depression. Jesus paid the price for you to walk free. When I walk in victory, I am walking in what the Blood of Jesus paid for. It's already paid for! You already have it! You must choose to walk in it intentionally. I love this verse. David encouraged AND strengthened himself in the Lord. Not in movies, music, friends, or anything else, but in the Lord. The ultimate source of strength. And His strength is here for you today!

And David enquired at the LORD, saying, Shall I pursue after this troop? shall I overtake them? And he answered him, Pursue: for thou shalt surely overtake them, and without fail recover all.

I SAMUEL 30:8 KJV

You *will* recover all! That word is for you and any believer daring to believe God's Word is true. You will recover everything you've lost. What the devil stole from you will be paid back in full! All doesn't mean a little bit or a portion. It means you will recover *everything* due to you. David still had to go to battle. David went to battle, and the Word of the Lord did not return void.

VICTORIOUS IN BATTLE

David recovered all that the Amalekites had taken and rescued his two wives. Nothing was missing, small or great, sons or daughters, spoil or anything that had been taken; David recovered all. Also David captured all the flocks and herds [which the enemy had], and the people drove those animals before him and said, This is David's spoil.

1 SAMUEL 30:18-20 AMPC

David recovered all. For us, getting on that plane to Europe was our battlefield. For you, that's going to be different. Inquire of the Lord, and ask Him for help, strength, and encouragement. If He did it for David and He did it for me, He *will* do it for you.

I want you to read Psalm 18. Meditate on it and get it in your spirit. Below is an exercise I did that will help you get into that place of victory. Grab a piece of paper and make three columns titled: God, Me, and the devil. Read this Psalm, and list the following:

1. Each characteristic of God.
2. What God wants you to do.
3. What David did.
4. What looks like the devil and his works.

Take time to read through the scripture carefully. Take a few days, if necessary, but read it repeatedly, and don't rush through it. As you get into God's Word, His Word will get into you, and you'll become one with it.

To the Chief Musician. [A Psalm] of David the servant of the Lord, who spoke the words of this song to the Lord on the day when the Lord delivered him from the hand of all his enemies and from the hand of Saul. And he said:

I love You fervently and devotedly, O Lord, my Strength.
The Lord is my Rock, my Fortress, and my Deliverer; my God, my keen and firm Strength in Whom I will trust and take refuge, my Shield, and the Horn of my salvation, my High Tower.
I will call upon the Lord, Who is to be praised; so shall I be saved from my enemies.
The cords or bands of death surrounded me, and the streams of ungodliness and the torrents of ruin terrified me.
The cords of Sheol (the place of the dead) surrounded me; the snares of death confronted and came upon me.
In my distress [when seemingly closed in] I called upon the Lord and cried to my God; He heard my voice out of His temple (heavenly dwelling place), and my cry came before Him, into His [very] ears.
Then the earth quaked and rocked, the foundations also of the mountains trembled; they moved and were shaken because He was indignant and angry.
There went up smoke from His nostrils; and lightning out of His mouth devoured; coals were kindled by it.
He bowed the heavens also and came down; and thick darkness was under His feet.
And He rode upon a cherub [a storm] and flew [swiftly]; yes, He sped on with the wings of the wind.

VICTORIOUS IN BATTLE

He made darkness His secret hiding place; as His pavilion (His canopy) round about Him were dark waters and thick clouds of the skies.

Out of the brightness before Him there broke forth through His thick clouds hailstones and coals of fire. The Lord also thundered from the heavens, and the Most High uttered His voice, amid hailstones and coals of fire.

And He sent out His arrows and scattered them; and He flashed forth lightnings and put them to rout.

Then the beds of the sea appeared and the foundations of the world were laid bare at Your rebuke, O Lord, at the blast of the breath of Your nostrils.

He reached from on high, He took me; He drew me out of many waters.

He delivered me from my strong enemy and from those who hated and abhorred me, for they were too strong for me.

They confronted and came upon me in the day of my calamity, but the Lord was my stay and support.

He brought me forth also into a large place; He was delivering me because He was pleased with me and delighted in me.

The Lord rewarded me according to my righteousness (my conscious integrity and sincerity with Him); according to the cleanness of my hands has He recompensed me.

For I have kept the ways of the Lord and have not wickedly departed from my God.

For all His ordinances were before me, and I put not away His statutes from me.

I was upright before Him and blameless with Him,

ever [on guard] to keep myself free from my sin and guilt.

Therefore has the Lord recompensed me according to my righteousness (my uprightness and right standing with Him), according to the cleanness of my hands in His sight.

With the kind and merciful You will show Yourself kind and merciful, with an upright man You will show Yourself upright,

With the pure You will show Yourself pure, and with the perverse You will show Yourself contrary.

For You deliver an afflicted and humble people but will bring down those with haughty looks.

For You cause my lamp to be lighted and to shine; the Lord my God illumines my darkness.

For by You I can run through a troop, and by my God I can leap over a wall.

As for God, His way is perfect! The word of the Lord is tested and tried; He is a shield to all those who take refuge and put their trust in Him.

For who is God except the Lord? Or who is the Rock save our God,

The God who girds me with strength and makes my way perfect?

He makes my feet like hinds' feet [able to stand firmly or make progress on the dangerous heights of testing and trouble]; He sets me securely upon my high places.

He teaches my hands to war, so that my arms can bend a bow of bronze.

You have also given me the shield of Your salvation, and Your right hand has held me up; Your gentleness and condescension have made me great.

VICTORIOUS IN BATTLE

You have given plenty of room for my steps under me, that my feet would not slip.
I pursued my enemies and overtook them; neither did I turn again till they were consumed.
I smote them so that they were not able to rise; they fell wounded under my feet.
For You have girded me with strength for the battle; You have subdued under me and caused to bow down those who rose up against me.
You have also made my enemies turn their backs to me, that I might cut off those who hate me.
They cried [for help], but there was none to deliver—even unto the Lord, but He answered them not.
Then I beat them small as the dust before the wind; I emptied them out as the dirt and mire of the streets.
You have delivered me from the strivings of the people; You made me the head of the nations; a people I had not known served me.
As soon as they heard of me, they obeyed me; foreigners submitted themselves cringingly and yielded feigned obedience to me.
Foreigners lost heart and came trembling out of their caves or strongholds.
The Lord lives! Blessed be my Rock; and let the God of my salvation be exalted,
The God Who avenges me and subdues peoples under me,
Who delivers me from my enemies; yes, You lift me up above those who rise up against me; You deliver me from the man of violence.
Therefore will I give thanks and extol You, O Lord, among the nations, and sing praises to Your name.
Great deliverances and triumphs gives He to His king;

*and He shows mercy and steadfast love to His
anointed, to David and his offspring forever.*

Psalm 18 AMPC

Once you are done, look at who has the longest list. Not only does God do the most; He has the most power. It was powerful seeing how big God is, how small the devil is, and the lack of power the devil has. Once you see it too, your perspective will never be the same.

CHAPTER SIX

THE WEAPON

Turn Past Pains into Glorious Weapons to Fight the Devil

Why would you want to live defeated? That won't help anyone. I've been in both places, and you don't want to live in defeat. Psalm 30:5 tells us "...Weeping may endure for the night, but JOY comes in the morning." What a good reminder. Although we go through things, we can *still* have joy. There is a time to weep, mourn, and cry, but there is also a time to overcome. There is a time to rise above and be strong.

> *For our light, momentary affliction (this slight distress of the passing hour) is ever more and more abundantly preparing and producing and achieving for us an everlasting weight of glory [beyond all measure, excessively surpassing all comparisons and all calculations, a vast and transcendent glory and blessedness never to cease!],*
>
> 2 Corinthians 4:17 AMPC

> **You have an everlasting weight of glory waiting for you. Don't give that up for pain and pity parties. I would rather walk in His glory than stay in a trap set by the devil, making me ineffective.**

At the age of five, my husband lost his father to suicide. Early in our relationship, I was sitting with his mom, discussing what happened. She said, "If I had to go through everything I went through to help one person, I would do it all again." This was so powerful and profound, and I live by it. I never had that perspective on tough situations and circumstances. No woman wants to lose her husband and be a widow with fatherless children. No woman wants to miscarry and almost die. The reality is that it happened, and now, we must choose what we will do. Will we wallow in pain and self-pity, or will we rise?

I wanted to rise. I wanted to help other people, and I didn't have a choice. I *had to* because I felt the Holy Spirit tell me to! If it were up to me, I would have kept the attack we went through very quiet. I would not have told anyone unless I had to, but the Holy Spirit led me to share it. In Finland, we recorded a video of what happened and released it when we returned home. It touched many lives. Many unexpected women who also had miscarriages contacted me, sharing that our story brought them hope and healing. Someone must step up and have victory in an area. Sometimes, you must be the first person. By having victory, you'll pave the way, helping to lead others into their victory.

I love the story of David and Goliath. David went to the battlefield and saw the Israelite army being mocked by the Philistines. No one was brave enough to stand up, or willing to take on Goliath. David saw this and was led by the Lord to take him on. They tried to give David Saul's armor, but that didn't work.

> **You can never do what God has for you, trying to be someone God hasn't called you to be.**

When David picked up those five smooth stones, he picked up the equipping the Lord had for him and no one else. He defeated Goliath, and then cut off his head with Goliath's sword as we see in 1 Samuel:

Therefore David ran, and stood upon the Philistine, and took his sword, and drew it out of the sheath thereof, and slew him, and cut off his head therewith. And when the Philistines saw their champion was dead, they fled.

1 SAMUEL 17:51 KJV

This is a great example of having a battle, but turning the battle into a weapon. As 1 Samuel progresses, David fought other battles.

David said to Ahimelech, Do you have at hand a sword or spear? The king's business required haste, and I brought neither my sword nor my weapons with me. The priest said, The sword of Goliath the Philistine, whom you slew in the Valley of Elah, see, it is here wrapped in a cloth behind the ephod; if you will take that, do so, for there is no other here. And David said, There is none like that; give it to me. David arose and fled that day from Saul and went to Achish king of Gath.

1 Samuel 21:8-10 AMPC

David took the sword he used to cut off Goliath's head and used it to protect himself when fighting for his life against Saul. This gives you permission to take an attack, get victory, and use it to help set yourself and other people free.

Throughout the years, I would randomly feel like I needed to share my testimony on social media, and each time I did, someone would say, "You shared that for me. I was struggling, and this helped me so much." There is power in your testimony. You must understand that your testimony can and will help set others free. This is what the Word says about the power of your testimony in Revelation:

And they have overcome (conquered) him by means of the blood of the Lamb and by the utterance of their testimony, for they did not love and cling to life even when faced with death [holding their lives cheap till they had to die for their witnessing].

Revelation 12:11 AMPC

Below are additional verses about the power of your testimony to encourage you:

And with great strength and ability and power the apostles delivered their testimony to the resurrection of the Lord Jesus, and great grace (loving-kindness and favor and goodwill) rested richly upon them all.

ACTS 4:33 AMPC

Return to your home, and recount [the story] of how many and great things God has done for you. And [the man] departed, proclaiming throughout the whole city how much Jesus had done for him.

LUKE 8:39 AMPC

I will praise You, O Lord, with my whole heart; I will show forth (recount and tell aloud) all Your marvelous works and wonderful deeds!

PSALM 9:1 AMPC

The devil would love to see you go through something, be defeated, and never recover. Don't give him that satisfaction. I haven't been through what you have, but someone else has and needs to see you walk in victory and hear your testimony. You are the key to someone else's breakthrough.

I overcame a miscarriage, and if that's your story, you can too. You can overcome any situation you're facing right now, whether it's in your body, family, ministry, business, work, or finances. I am living proof, and you can do it too.

> **Whatever area of your life has been attacked, from this moment, I give you permission to break through. You can and will have victory in every area of your life.**

God's Word calls you victorious! Below are scriptures and confessions for you to say out loud daily, for a life of perpetual victory. I pray you declare God's Word with unwavering faith and boldness, knowing that He is "alert *and* active, watching over His word to perform it" (Jeremiah 1:12 AMPC).

Body

> *But He said to me, My grace (My favor and lovingkindness and mercy) is enough for you [sufficient against any danger and enables you to bear the trouble manfully]; for My strength and power are made perfect (fulfilled and completed) and show themselves most effective in [your] weakness. Therefore, I will all the more gladly glory in my weaknesses and infirmities, that the strength and power of Christ (the Messiah) may rest (yes, may pitch a tent over and dwell) upon me!*

2 Corinthians 12:9 AMPC

Confession: His grace is sufficient for me. My strength and power are made perfect in His weakness. I will glory in the strength that Christ made available to me. I dwell in His strength, so my body is strong.

Mind

For God hath not given us the spirit of fear; but of power, and of love, and of a sound mind.

2 TIMOTHY 1:7 KJV

Confession: I do not fear. I have power, love, and a sound mind.

Spirit

A happy heart is good medicine and a cheerful mind works healing, but a broken spirit dries up the bones.

PROVERBS 17:22 AMPC

Confession: My heart is happy and acts like a medicine. I'm cheerful and my body is whole. My spirit is not broken.

Soul

Beloved, I pray that you may prosper in every way and [that your body] may keep well, even as [I know] your soul keeps well and prospers.

3 JOHN 1:2 AMPC

Confession: I prosper in every way. I am well, and my soul is well and prospers.

Health

> *Do you not know that your body is the temple (the very sanctuary) of the Holy Spirit Who lives within you, Whom you have received [as a Gift] from God? You are not your own, You were bought with a price [purchased with a preciousness and paid for, made His own]. So then, honor God and bring glory to Him in your body.*
>
> 1 Corinthians 6:19-20 AMPC

Confession: I was bought with a price. He paid for me, so I bring glory to Him in my body. I am healthy and completely whole.

Wealth

> *And Abram was very rich in cattle, in silver, and in gold.*
>
> Genesis 13:2 KJV

Confession: Just as Abram was very rich, so am I. Wealth and riches belong to me.

Business

Do you see a man diligent and skillful in his business? He will stand before kings; he will not stand before obscure men.

Proverbs 22:29 AMPC

Confession: I am diligent and skillful in my business, so I will stand before kings. Men and women of great prominence will seek my God-given skills and talents. I am a solution center to my generation.

Salvation

For whosoever shall call upon the name of the Lord shall be saved.

Romans 10:13 KJV

Confession: I have assurance of my salvation because I call on His Name.

Lost loved ones being saved

The Lord is not slack concerning his promise, as some men count slackness; but is longsuffering to us-ward, not willing that any should perish, but that all should come to repentance.

2 Peter 3:9 KJV

Confession: The Lord does not slack concerning His promises. He is not willing that anyone perish, but that all should come to repentance, even my family members. Father, I thank You that my family members are saved and living on fire for You in Jesus' Name.

Strength

But those who wait for the Lord [who expect, look for, and hope in Him] shall change and renew their strength and power; they shall lift their wings and mount up [close to God] as eagles [mount up to the sun]; they shall run and not be weary, they shall walk and not faint or become tired.

Isaiah 40:31 AMPC

Confession: I wait on the Lord, and He renews my strength and power. I run, and I'm not weary. I walk, and I am not faint or tired.

Being strong in old age

Even to your old age I am He, and even to hair white with age will I carry you. I have made, and I will bear; yes, I will carry and will save you.

Isaiah 46:4 AMPC

VICTORIOUS IN BATTLE

Moses was 120 years old when he died; his eye was not dim nor his natural force abated.

DEUTERONOMY 34:7 KJV

Confession: God will carry me, bear me, and save me as I age. My eyes do not dim, and my natural force is not abated.

Relationships

A man that hath friends must shew himself friendly: and there is a friend that sticketh closer than a brother.

PROVERBS 18:24 KJV

Therefore encourage one another and build each other up, just as in fact you are doing.

I THESSALONIANS 5:11 NIV

Confession: I have friends who stick closer than brothers. We encourage one another and build each other up.

Marriage

Iron sharpens iron; so a man sharpens the countenance of his friend [to show rage or worthy purpose].

PROVERBS 27:17 AMPC

Confession: My marriage makes both of us sharper. Together, we are getting better, and we are an unstoppable team advancing God's Kingdom.

Infertility

Then God remembered Rachel and answered her pleading and made it possible for her to have children.

GENESIS 30:22 AMPC

Confession: God makes it possible for me to have children. I will safely conceive, carry, and birth healthy children. I will raise my children according to God's Word, and they will be used mightily to advance God's Kingdom.

Future/Destiny

For I know the thoughts and plans that I have for you, says the Lord, thoughts and plans for welfare and peace and not for evil, to give you hope in your final outcome.

JEREMIAH 29:11 AMPC

Before I formed you in the womb I knew you [and approved of you as My chosen instrument], And before you were born I consecrated you [to Myself as My own]; I have appointed you as a prophet to the nations.

JEREMIAH 1:5 AMP

But the path of the just (righteous) is like the light of dawn, That shines brighter and brighter until [it reaches its full strength and glory in] the perfect day.

PROVERBS 4:18 AMP

Now the Lord is that Spirit: and where the Spirit of the Lord is, there is liberty. But we all, with open face beholding as in a glass the glory of the Lord, are changed into the same image from glory to glory, even as by the Spirit of the Lord.

2 CORINTHIANS 3:17-18 KJV

Confession: He knows the thoughts and plans He has for me. He has plans of peace and to give me a good outcome. He knew and approved me as His chosen instrument. I shine brighter and brighter. I am changed from glory to glory.

Unity

Behold, how good and how pleasant it is for brethren to dwell together in unity! It is like the precious ointment poured on the head, that ran down on the beard, even the beard of Aaron [the first high priest], that came down upon the collar and skirts of his garments [consecrating the whole body].

PSALM 133:1-2 AMPC

How could one have chased a thousand, and two have put ten thousand to flight, unless their Rock had sold them, and the Lord had given them up?

DEUTERONOMY 32:30 KJV

Confession: It is pleasant for us to dwell in unity. One can put one thousand to flight, and two can put ten thousand.

Forgiveness

Then came Peter to him, and said, Lord, how oft shall my brother sin against me, and I forgive him? till seven times? Jesus saith unto him, I say not unto thee, Until seven times: but, Until seventy times seven.

MATTHEW 18:21-22 KJV

But if you do not forgive others their trespasses [their reckless and willful sins, leaving them, letting them go, and giving up resentment], neither will your Father forgive you your trespasses.

MATTHEW 6:15 AMPC

Confession: I forgive seventy times seven. I forgive so He can forgive me. I leave no room in my heart for unforgiveness or offense.

Sleep

> *When you lie down, you shall not be afraid; yes, you shall lie down, and your sleep shall be sweet.*
>
> PROVERBS 3:24 AMPC

Confession: When I lie down, my sleep is sweet.

Pregnancy

> *And God blessed them and said to them, Be fruitful, multiply, and fill the earth, and subdue it [using all its vast resources in the service of God and man]; and have dominion over the fish of the sea, the birds of the air, and over every living creature that moves upon the earth.*
>
> GENESIS 1:28 AMPC

Confession: We are fruitful and multiplying like God intended in His original plan.

Children

> *Children are a heritage from the Lord, offspring a reward from him. Like arrows in the hands of a*

warrior are children born in one's youth. Blessed is the man whose quiver is full of them. They will not be put to shame when they contend with their opponents in court.

> PSALM 127:3-5 NIV

Confession: My children are my heritage and reward.

There are more areas, but these are just a few. My husband and I have succeeded in business, and I know that has inspired others to do the same, or take territory in other areas. God is no respecter of persons.

For God shows no partiality [undue favor or unfairness; with Him one man is not different from another].

> ROMANS 2:11 AMPC

What He has done for us, He will surely do for you. We each have different areas we need to conquer. What is that area for you? What is the area that frustrates you? What is the area you feel like you could change? That's most likely the area God wants to use you in. I think it's wrong that so many women have infertility issues and miscarriages. So this is the area He is using me in. I want to see moms have a joyful motherhood, the way God intended.

VICTORIOUS IN BATTLE

He makes the barren woman to be a homemaker and a joyful mother of [spiritual] children. Praise the Lord! (Hallelujah!)

PSALM 113:9 AMPC

He intends for me to be a joyful mother. You don't need 100 scriptures to feel like something in the Word is yours. It took one Man, one sacrifice, and one resurrection to give me access to all that is available to me. If it's in the Word, take it as yours.

I haven't done everything I desire concerning motherhood, but this is a start. I also want to see people live up to their full potential and walk in victory. I love what Brother Kenneth E. Hagin says, "I'm not there yet, but I'm on the way."

It's okay if you aren't where you want to be yet. It's okay if there are areas you still need to grow in. It's okay if your realm of influence isn't as big as you want it to be. But what can you do now? Where can you start now? What can you be faithful with now? A lot of people don't start anything or share their victories because they are stopped by a limiting mindset.

Take the limitations off. I'm not an expert, but I am a willing vessel. I am willing and obedient to do what I feel the Lord is calling me to do. Sometimes, being willing is more important than having the skill. David killed a lion and bear, but according to Saul's standard, he was not the man for the job.

Do not despise these small beginnings, for the Lord rejoices to see the work begin, to see the plumb line in Zerubbabel's hand." (The seven lamps represent the eyes of the Lord that search all around the world.)

ZECHARIAH 4:10 NLT

The Lord rejoices when He sees you working at what He has placed in your heart to do! Whatever you have been called to do, be faithful. Everyone wants to be the powerful king, but no one wants to be the shepherd. In reality, the shepherd is more in tune with what the flock needs. The shepherd is seen as having a lower job, but the most important job is the one He has called you to do. We are each graced and equipped to complete different missions.

> **You have a mission from Heaven, and God has a testimony in mind for you. He isn't calling you to do something and fail. He is calling you to His perfect purpose to succeed.**

When God thought of you, He planned a special position for you in His army. He didn't make you and say, I don't know what I am going to do with that one. He planned a purpose for you:

For I know the thoughts and plans that I have for you, says the Lord, thoughts and plans for welfare and peace and not for evil, to give you hope in your final outcome.

JEREMIAH 29:11 AMPC

You might not feel, believe, or see it, but it's true. The only difference between a victim and victor is their mindset. A survivor of the Holocaust could say, "What a terrible thing they did to me," and be a victim, or they can say, "Look at what I was saved from. I did not succumb to those situations and circumstances. I rose above." Every day, the choice is ours.

I don't feel I am the most qualified person to write a book. I am sure there were others God called, but they didn't answer. But you are holding the obedience of what God called me to do. Four times a year, our church has campmeetings. Two meetings a day for eight days. It would be so easy to say, "There is another one in a few months. I can just attend that one and take this time off." If anyone has an excuse, it would be my husband and I. We travel a lot for work, and sometimes, we were gone for half of the year. But we always made getting in God's presence and anointing our priority. Sometimes, we'd even fly in for that week and leave the next. We know whatever God has for us during those campmeetings, we can only get it at that time. It's our time to level up, and we can't miss those opportunities.

The best way to get stronger is to get in the presence of the Lord. As mentioned in Chapter Two, repetition reaps results. Consistently sharing your testimony, reading the Word, winning souls, going to church, and getting in anointed meetings, where the Holy Spirit is free to move, changes you from glory to glory. Don't just share your testimony once. Share it with anyone it will encourage.

> **Your testimony is your weapon. It's what tells the devil where you stand.**

It tells the devil he can not attack or defeat you. If you are pressed, share the testimony God has given you.

One time, my husband felt to do an altar call in his sales office, but he felt a little timid because of the vast array of people with different religious backgrounds. He was sure it was going to end in a call to Human Resources. I was in Orlando for a good friend's baby shower with our daughter Eva. His mom was supposed to visit us, as we had been traveling for weeks for work and still had many weeks to go. We were only in town for the day, and this was our only opportunity to see her.

Tim's mom called and she said she wasn't feeling well and wouldn't be able to see us. A Holy anger rose in my husband, and he said, "Mom, you can't let the devil bully you. If you let him push you now, he is going to try again. Set an alarm, take a rest, then get up and get ready, and go to that baby shower." Tim was so mad at the devil for attacking his mom. He walked into the sales meeting, did an altar call, and the whole office prayed the prayer of salvation, including people with differing religious beliefs. Tim's mom met us at the baby shower, and we had a lovely day with her.

> **Every test, trial, or pain can be used for victory.**

One of my good friends is an evangelist who always says, "You must live out of your spirit." What does that mean? When you are under the anointing, what is the thing you feel God telling you to do? Usually, whatever it is, you feel inadequate to do it when you get into your "normal" everyday life. But living from your spirit is acting on what you feel to do when you are under the anointing. David might not have felt anointed to kill Goliath, but he had to act on what God told him to do. Attack, fight, and win! Never back down, and never let a defeat dictate who you are or what you do.

CHAPTER SEVEN

THE TESTIMONY

Judah's Birth Story

After we returned from Europe, we took some time to reset. We took time as a family to be together and strengthen our foundation. Our church has a healing school, which we attended. In January 2018, we felt ready to try for our next baby. My husband and I agreed on the timing, and we were pregnant our first month of trying. I applied the same confessions and principles I used with Eva. I went for my ten-week appointment, and they said I was measuring early. I went in for an ultrasound, and they decided to move my due date up a week.

This pregnancy mirrored my pregnancy with Eva. I had the same food aversions and cravings. I wanted potatoes in any form and chocolate milkshakes. I traveled much more during this pregnancy than I did with Eva, but God graced us all for the task at hand. Especially my husband, who had to do all the heavy lifting of our luggage. We had a gender reveal at twenty weeks, and learned I was carrying our son, Judah. His name means praise. We chose the names Eva and Judah during my first pregnancy before knowing what we were having. I think it's amazing God led us to name our kids life (Eva) and praise (Judah). In our darkest moment, we praised God, and we were consistently reminded with our son's name.

What you name your kids matters. What you confess matters, so the meaning of your children's names matter. It is what you are speaking over them, so choose wisely. Let the Lord lead you in naming your children.

Back to the story of Judah. The whole time, I remember feeling like he was sitting so low. I remember flying into Houston and taking it easy the entire week because I felt he could've come at any moment. Weeks went by, and Eva and I returned home a few weeks before Tim. I was about thirty-six to thirty-seven weeks, and Eva and I were at Costco. Suddenly, I started feeling like my labor could've been starting. With Eva, I had no sign or warning. It just started and didn't stop. I called my husband and asked him to pray for me. He prayed our son would not be born until the time the Lord had appointed for him, and I instantly felt better. I spent the last few weeks ensuring everything was in order, because usually, second babies come earlier than the first ones *and* faster. Since he was sitting so low, I knew he would come early.

I ensured our house was in order, the car seat was installed, and made lots of freezer meals. Around that time, we had a wedding we were performing, and my RSVP was, "*I'll be there as long as I am not having a baby.*" So thirty-eight weeks came and went, thirty-nine weeks came and went, and when we got to forty weeks, I was sure he would come, but he didn't. At forty-one weeks, I became more emotional. In Florida, you must be in active labor at forty-two weeks on the day, or you have to go to the hospital and be induced.

For most women, that's not a big deal. However, that's not what I wanted at all. I wanted to be at the birth center with the same midwife who delivered Eva. My sister flew into town to help me, and I remember being so upset Judah had not arrived. I told her, "I am so sorry he isn't here." She said, "Well, it is not your fault. He will come when he is ready." My sister worked in Mother & Baby Care for many years, and had seen a lot of good and bad outcomes. I was excited for her to see a supernatural birth...as long as he would come out.

At forty-one weeks and a few days, I did an ultrasound and took a nonstress test. I wondered what he could possibly be doing. The ultrasound and nonstress test went great. He was perfect, and the umbilical cord was in a great position. There was no reason in the natural he was not coming out. The midwives asked me if I wanted to do natural things, like stripping my membranes to get labor going, and I didn't know what to do. With the amount of estrogen flowing, everything seemed like a big deal.

My husband was there, and I said, "I don't know what to do." He said, "Well, the Lord has brought us this far with a perfect pregnancy. I want our testimony to be that we let God do what He needed to do, and our baby came forth in His perfect time." After our appointment, we went and ate tacos and walked on the beach.

My sister was in town for two weeks, so we decided to make the most of every moment, regardless of my labor progress. That night, I took the pressure off, cried a little, and went to sleep. We woke up and planned to go to brunch. That morning, some contractions started, but I didn't want to say anything. As we ate, my contractions picked up. We stopped at a local coffee shop, and I got a spiced pumpkin latte. I thought to myself, "*I will probably throw this up later*," but got one anyway. We went to the mall, and as we walked around, my contractions picked up more and more. I finally told my husband and sister I was having contractions. I started timing them and realized how close together they were. I said, "When they get a minute closer, we should probably leave."

I knew how my labor progressed with Eva, and this one seemed to be following the same pattern, only faster. We decided it was probably best to head to the birth center. We stopped in Nordstrom to use the bathroom, and I lost my mucus plug. I knew this baby was coming fast! I knew my water would break soon, and so at the fanciest section in the department store, we asked for some bags to put down on our car seats. With horror in their eyes, *at the idea of my water breaking on their floor*, they threw garments bags at us and rushed us out of the store. It was a Friday afternoon, and we knew we needed to get there quickly to avoid rush hour.

We arrived at the birth center before the nurse and midwives. I had a letter board and put the date on it while we waited for them to arrive. It was October 12, 2018. We arrived around 4 p.m. The midwife checked me. I was 7 centimeters dilated and 80 percent effaced. I knew I was there earlier than with Eva, but I didn't want to give birth on the side of the road. My sister was with Eva, and then my mother-in-love, Veronique, arrived so my sister could come watch the birth. Veronique witnessed Eva's delivery and said it was one of the greatest gifts of her life. She really wanted to attend the birth of Judah as well.

Tim kept saying, "You need to get in the tub," with the same attitude as when I was in labor with Eva. I didn't understand why he was being so pushy and rushing me. I said, "Give me one more contraction." I remember seeing my midwife sitting on the floor, looking at me with such intensity. She obviously knew what was about to happen. At that moment, my water broke. I got in the tub and began pushing. Soon after, "Uncle and Auntie" (Tim's brother, Ryan, and his wife, Christa) arrived. Veronique rushed back to the delivery room, and Auntie Christa wanted to come say hello, not realizing where I was in the process. She peeked her head in, and there I was pushing. It was about twenty minutes of pushing total, and Judah arrived. Within about two hours of arriving, I was holding our precious baby boy.

My sister witnessed a birth unlike anything she had seen, and my mother-in-love also got to see her second grandchild born. Christa got her faith inspired to believe God for supernatural childbirth. She has since had three children, and wrote an amazing book, *Birth with Joy*, which I highly recommend for any pregnant ladies.

If I had given into fear, this story would have gone differently. Christa would probably not have had the birth experiences she did and written a book that, in a short time, has helped so many women. We would not have a testimony to share, and a true victory over the attack we faced. I feel like we saw the completion of the testimony that began when we lost our second child.

We are supposed to live in victory, and Judah's birth was a testimony of my living victory. Yes, there was a battle in between, but that's not where I stayed. We don't live on the battlefield. We are to live victorious in God. No one becomes strong fighting everyday. We go from glory to glory, victory to victory, strength to strength, and faith to faith. If the devil has challenged or attacked you, this is the moment to fight. This is the moment to turn that battle into victory.

Why would you want to move into a place of defeat? What's the story? *I had a tragic experience and lived there*? *I stayed there, and it defined me*? Or, I had a tragedy, and now God can use it for His glory. How? He can take anything and make it a weapon, using it to help set others free.

Judah's birth was my sweet victory and my reward. They call a baby that comes after a miscarriage a *rainbow baby*—a sign of God's promise. Judah is indeed my promise of God's will and His goodness. His way is better than any other. And yes, I did throw up that spiced pumpkin latte, in case you were wondering. But if that was the worst thing that happened, I will take it.

If I had given into fear, I could have opened myself up to more miscarriages and complications, but thank God I didn't. Opening yourself to fear will never reap anything good in your life, but remaining in faith will always reap blessings. I needed my husband by my side, supporting me in those final days of pregnancy, but I was not in fear. When I was mentally prepared for our boy to come early, and he didn't, it made my emotions much harder to manage. Having my husband there with me meant everything.

It's okay to need help and support. You don't have to go through life alone. In fact, you need strong people of faith in your life who will encourage you if you feel you need it. I needed my husband's strength, and that didn't make me weak. Desiring the help of others doesn't make you weak, either.

One of the biggest lies is that "a pregnant woman is *sick* and needs medical interventions." Some do for sure, but most do not. You simply need to be healthy, taking care of and educating yourself on what's best for you and your baby. I know many ladies who had membrane stripping done, but you have to follow what you feel the Holy Spirit telling *you* to do. I probably would have started interventions, but my husband's faith was at a different level—to see our baby come on his own, without medical interventions. We needed to see God work for us at that level, and He did exactly what we believed for.

Joshua 24 is such a good example of having a battle and a victory. We know the Israelites got the Promised Land, but there were giants in the land. There were many battles to face, and they had to act. They had to fully trust and rely on God with unwavering faith, and act on that faith.

> *I brought you into the land of the Amorites who lived on the other side of the Jordan; they fought with you, and I gave them into your hand, and you possessed their land, and I destroyed them before you. Then Balak son of Zippor, king of Moab, arose and warred against Israel, and sent and called Balaam son of Beor to curse you. But I would not listen to Balaam; therefore he blessed you; so I delivered you out of Balak's hand. You went over the Jordan and came to Jericho; and the men of Jericho fought against you, as did the Amorites, Perizzites, Canaanites, Hittites, Girgashites, Hivites, and Jebusites, and I gave them into your hands. I sent the hornet [that is, the terror of*

you] before you, which drove the two kings of the Amorites out before you; but it was not by your sword or by your bow. I have given you a land for which you did not labor and cities you did not build, and you dwell in them; you eat from vineyards and olive yards you did not plant. Now therefore, [reverently] fear the Lord and serve Him in sincerity and in truth; put away the gods which your fathers served on the other side of the [Euphrates] River and in Egypt, and serve the Lord.

JOSHUA 24:8-14 AMPC

Confess this now: I take territory. I do not hold back. I do not delay. I move forward with boldness and confidence. My confidence is in the Lord, and what He tells me to do. I will obey God's commands and have a glorious testimony. God has a testimony with my name on it. God is moving towards me with favor. All of my steps are ordered by the Lord.

CHAPTER EIGHT

SOUND MIND

What You Don't Discipline Will Dominate You

To be victorious in any area, you must be strong. If you want to be strong physically, you will have to work for it. And spiritually, there is a supernatural equipping by the Holy Spirit. He makes us strong. I love Psalm 18:29-30:

For by You I can run through a troop, and by my God I can leap over a wall. As for God, His way is perfect! The word of the Lord is tested and tried; He is a shield to all those who take refuge and put their trust in Him.

PSALM 18:29-30 AMPC

When we trust in Him, we can do supernatural things. Just like Elijah ran before Ahab, who was in a chariot.

And at the seventh time the servant said, A cloud as small as a man's hand is arising out of the sea. And Elijah said, Go up, say to Ahab, Hitch your chariot and go down, lest the rain stop you. In a little while, the heavens were black with wind-swept clouds, and there was a great rain. And Ahab went to Jezreel. The hand of the Lord was on Elijah. He girded up his loins and ran before Ahab to the entrance of Jezreel [nearly twenty miles].

1 KINGS 18:44-46 AMPC

Maybe Elijah wasn't in the gym strength-training everyday, but he was strong in the Lord. He knew His God, and the supernatural power available to him. It's crazy to me that people expect to be victorious and have no discipline. Even Jesus was tempted by the devil with the Word of God. In Matthew 4:1-11, we see the devil coming to Jesus three times and using the Word against Him. So we must know the Word and be strong in it. But we must also be strong in our bodies and in our minds. No matter where we face challenges, we have a promise to stand on.

For God hath not given us the spirit of fear; but of power, and of love, and of a sound mind.

2 TIMOTHY 1:7 KJV

Did you know you can have strength of mind? 1 Chronicles 5:24 says:

And these were the heads of their fathers' houses: Epher, Ishi, Eliel, Azriel, Jeremiah, Hodaviah, and

VICTORIOUS IN BATTLE

Jahdiel, mighty men of strength of mind and spirit [enabling them to encounter danger with firmness and personal bravery], famous men, and heads of the houses of their fathers.

1 CHRONICLES 5:24 AMPC

Confess this verse over yourself: I am a (man/woman) of strength of mind and spirit. I encounter danger with firmness and bravery.

Ultimately, these men were unfaithful to God, but there was a supernatural equipping of strength of mind. Too often, we get arrogant in our strength, thinking *we've made it*. Always know that it's the Lord. It's by His might, strength, and power we are able to do anything.

Then he said to me, "This is what the Lord says to Zerubbabel: It is not by force nor by strength, but by my Spirit, says the Lord of Heaven's Armies.

ZECHARIAH 4:6 NLT

We have the promise of a sound mind. What does a sound mind look like? I for one, think of victory! When I think of someone who is strong in their mind, it's definitely someone who isn't weak or wavering. My husband ran sales teams for fourteen-plus years. You talk about a tough job—outside in the heat, cold, rain, and snow. They worked early mornings and late nights. It didn't matter what was thrown at them, they *had* to work. Most of the battles were in their minds. It was their *own* beliefs. And there were three keys to a team's success:

1. Remaining teachable and trainable
2. Having a good attitude
3. Being a hard worker

If someone wasn't performing well, most of the issues came down to one of those key areas.

I do not think it's any different in our walk with the Lord. If we are ungrateful, He cannot bless us. If our attitude is bad, it's hard for Him to help us. If we are know-it-alls, or are unwilling to make adjustments, it's hard for Him to work with us. If we aren't willing to work, how can He bless us? He says He will bless the work of our hands.

The Lord shall open to you His good treasury, the heavens, to give the rain of your land in its season and to bless all the work of your hand; and you shall lend to many nations, but you shall not borrow.

Deuteronomy 28:12 KJV

With both my pregnancies and childbirths, I worked the Word. I put in so much time building up my faith, that there was no option for failure. **I was working.** A good friend even said to me, "You had really great births," and I said, "Yes." Then they said, "But you were working that whole pregnancy weren't you?" "Yes," I replied. I was reading, confessing, and upping my expectations and beliefs. This is not a book about birth. It is about you being equipped to go to war in any area with the Word, and it producing for you! **If you are weak in your mind, you will be weak in all you do.** Many people have wonderful ideas and could be some of the most successful people in business or ministry.

However, they doubt in their hearts and minds what God can do.

Sadly, today, there is a big push for mental health awareness without showing people how to overcome in this area. I dislike the focus being merely "awareness" of anything, because awareness doesn't bring change, nor does it bring strength. Do you know what brings strength? Being strong! Realizing you are not strong in an area, and then learning how to be better. Nowadays, people discuss their mental health issues or anxiety like it's a pet they carry around. People have emotional support dogs or pets. Your pet may decrease your anxiety, but it will not produce freedom or strengthen you mentally.

That's probably offensive, but it's true. Discussing your anxiety without biblical solutions glorifies the devil, making you weak. The Bible says "fear not" 365 times! God does not want you to fear. He wants you to be strong in the power of His might!

In conclusion, be strong in the Lord [be empowered through your union with Him]; draw your strength from Him [that strength which His boundless might provides].

Ephesians 6:10 AMPC

I know it's not always easy to be strong. I was shy, anxious, and full of fear and worry as a kid. In elementary school, I was so anxious about going to school, I started wetting the bed at night. I was a hypochondriac. Any little thing that happened turned into an overdramatic episode. I even had stomach problems due to anxiety. Since I didn't like school, I would also fake being sick so I wouldn't have to go. Then, in fourth grade, I got really sick and began vomiting up my stomach lining. My mom didn't believe me, and she had every reason not to. But this time, it was for real.

She made me go to church on a Wednesday night, and I remember laying in the nursery in pain. The next morning, she let me stay home from school, and I told her, "It hurts." She said, "What do you mean it hurts?" I said, "It hurts right there," pointing to my appendix. I was having an appendicitis attack. My mom's car was in the shop, and my dad was taking my sister to school. My mom called my grandmother, who lived around the corner, to take me to the hospital. My grandmother heard, "Simone is having an appendicitis attack," and drove straight to the hospital. She missed the part that we actually needed her to take us there. After a few minutes, my mom flagged down our neighbor, who drove us to the hospital.

I always hated needles and freaked out over them, but I was in so much pain, I didn't care. After running a few tests, it was confirmed I was having an appendicitis attack, and I needed an emergency appendectomy. They rushed me into surgery, and I never faked being sick EVER again!

As someone who has dealt with fear and anxiety as a child, what you believe and focus on is your choice. Whatever you focus on, good or bad, is what will be your portion. If you say, "Lord, that is not my portion," and get in the Word, finding scriptures to stand on and go to battle with, it's impossible for you to not be victorious. I have done it firsthand. Even today, when I workout or do something difficult, I'll tell myself, "I am strong, and I can do anything. I can do anything for thirty seconds, five minutes, or however long I need to do something that's challenging... I am more than a conqueror!" **I tell myself what the Word says, and that's what you must do.**

Life is far more difficult when you give in and focus on what's hard and what's negative. Even with homeschooling my daughter, we have had a few rough days. I had a revelation: A battle doesn't mean you have a bad life. It means you have an area to improve and get stronger in. I have a wonderful life, but everyday, I get to homeschool my daughter, which can be challenging. But it's good to be stretched, and it's good to grow. You will never grow if you don't do anything that challenges you.

I pray you get some grit and some fight in you, and I pray you get stronger. I pray you take the Word and make It yours. If you have any area of weakness in your mind, get strong through God's Word. As Martin Luther said:

> *"You can't stop the birds from flying over your head, but you can stop them from making a nest in your hair."*

Thoughts may come, and opportunities to grow and get stronger will happen in life, but know you are graced and equipped to handle them. For years, I felt I was an inadequate wife. Throughout our lives and marriage, things have not been a cakewalk. Not because we have a bad marriage, but because my husband and I haven't asked for an easy life. We asked for a life that's *worth it*. Often, there is little satisfaction in things that are easy. So my husband and I have always pushed ourselves to grow in every area we can.

Because of this, my husband has carried more pressure or stress than the average person. It's his job to cast those cares on the Lord, but I wanted to help him and didn't know how. I'd say, "I don't know how to help him or connect with him on this level." So it was hard, I struggled, and he didn't have the help he needed from me. Then, one day, I changed my perspective and my confession. I have always said, "God gave me my kids, and I am the perfect mom for them, and they are the perfect kids for me. God gives me specific wisdom on how to raise them." I took that same confession and applied it to my husband. I would say, "God gave me Tim to be my husband, so I am the perfect wife for him, and he is the perfect husband for me. Therefore, I know how to help him and how to be a strength to him. When he is around me, he is infused with strength."

Take any situation and begin to say what you want to see. The world was framed with the Words of God. He spoke, and everything we see and enjoy today was created. What you say matters. What you think and meditate upon matters. Your life is too costly and precious to live in anything less than God's absolute best for you. He paid the ultimate price, and He has an amazing plan for you. Confessing what you see, feel, or think in the natural will not yield the desired results. But boldly proclaiming what you see with the eyes of your spirit and acting on it will. We have seen it firsthand in our family, business, and ministry.

Why your confessions matter:

Death and life are in the power of the tongue: And they that love it shall eat the fruit thereof.

PROVERBS 18:21 KJV

Set a guard, O Lord, before my mouth; keep watch at the door of my lips.

PSALM 141:3 AMPC

He who guards his mouth keeps his life, but he who opens wide his lips comes to ruin.

PROVERBS 13:3 AMPC

The heart of the godly thinks carefully before speaking; the mouth of the wicked overflows with evil words.

PROVERBS 15:28 NLT

He who guards his mouth and his tongue keeps himself from troubles.

PROVERBS 21:23 AMPC

What you think is what you say, what you say is what you act upon, and what you act upon is what your life will become. If you want to be a better mom, confess you are the best mom for your kids. If you want to be a better spouse, confess you are the best one for your spouse. If you want to excel in your career, you have to speak what you want to see.

Through faith we understand that the worlds were framed by the word of God, so that things which are seen were not made of things which do appear.

HEBREWS 11:3 KJV

By God's Words, our whole Earth was framed. What you confess today is what you will see tomorrow, so what are you framing? If you think mentally weak thoughts, and start speaking them, that's what you will see. If you see yourself as strong, think yourself strong, and confess God's Word, which says you are strong, you will walk in God's supernatural strength.

There must be a level of discipline in your life. What you do not discipline in your life will dominate you. It might be food, exercise, laziness, distractions, social media, or thoughts. My dad always says this about raising kids, "You have to be disciplined about discipline." Identify any area of weakness and make a plan to go to war against it. I find the best way to do this is to make a schedule consisting of daily disciplines. Be realistic. Target one area, then move to another when you have it down consistently. It can be a small step, but take a step. Routines or schedules can be powerful tools. Of course, we have off days or days we must be flexible, but when you discipline your time, you realize how much time you have wasted. Idle minds have time to focus on worry, but someone who is busy has no time to worry.

I am not perfect, but I am willing, and I am also growing. I strive to know Him more and grow everyday, and I pray this book has inspired you to do the same. I pray you have been encouraged, that your faith has increased, and that you have a revelation on areas you can grow and improve in. I hope you see that anything you face is not something you face alone, but with the Sword, which is the living Word of God and the Holy Spirit. God left us our Intercessor and our Standby. He left us with a Comforter. David encouraged himself in the Lord, but now, the Holy Spirit can come live big inside *you*. So, what greater things can you accomplish with what you have been given?

My prayer and heart's desire is that each person reading this book will step into the fullness of what God has for your life.

Confess this out loud over your life: I go from glory to glory, victory to victory, strength to strength, and faith to faith. I increase in victorious power. I increase in the One who has the power. When He calls, I believe, act, and obey. I am *Victorious In Battle*.

SALVATION

If you have never received Jesus Christ as your personal Lord and Savior, or you feel you need to make a fresh commitment to Him, say this prayer aloud:

Dear Lord Jesus, come into my heart. Forgive me of my sin. Wash me and cleanse me. Set me free. Jesus, thank You that You died for me. I believe that You are risen from the dead and that You're coming back again for me. Fill me with the Holy Spirit. Give me a passion for the lost, a hunger for the things of God, and a holy boldness to preach the gospel of Jesus Christ. I'm saved; I'm born again, I'm forgiven, and I'm on my way to Heaven because I have Jesus in my heart.

As a minister of the Gospel of Jesus Christ, I tell you today that all of your sins are forgiven. Always remember to run to God and not from God because He loves you and has a great plan for your life.

SALVATION

Your next steps are:

1. Get in a Bible-believing and teaching church, where the Holy Spirit is free to move.
2. Read your Bible and pray everyday.
3. Get filled with the Holy Spirit, if you aren't already.
4. Listen and act upon what the Holy Spirit tells you to do.

This might mean attending a Bible school or moving to a new city with a better church. Whatever it is, listen, follow, and obey. Intentionally take the steps needed to grow your relationship with God, build your faith, and live in His divine victory.

ABOUT THE AUTHOR

Simone is a fun and faith-filled wife and mom, and family is her greatest accomplishment. She gets much joy in working alongside her husband, Tim, being his greatest support and cheerleader. She loves homeschooling her children and raising them in the things of God.

Aside from leading a successful business together, they are equipping people to live victoriously personally, in ministry, and in business. Simone wants to see people catapulted from a life of defeat, to a life of unwavering faith, joy, and unending victory in every area! Her desire is for all moms to be full of joy and walk in the fullness of everything God has for them.

www.SIMONEJOOSTE.com

facebook.com/simonejoostebooks
instagram.com/simonejooste